The Faith of
BILLY GRAHAM

The Faith of
BILLY GRAHAM

❧

Compiled and Edited by Trudy S. Settel
Introduction by Cort R. Flint

TESTAMENT BOOKS
NEW YORK

This 2006 edition is published by Testament Books, an imprint of
Random House Value Publishing, a division of Random House, Inc., New York,
by arrangement with Settel Associates, Inc.

Testament is a registered trademark and the colophon is
a trademark of Random House, Inc.

Random House
New York • Toronto • London • Sydney • Auckland
www.randomhouse.com

Printed and bound in the United States of America.

A catalog record for this title is available from the Library of Congress.

ISBN 0-517-12430-0

10 9 8 7 6 5 4 3 2

CONCERNING THE
FAITH OF BILLY GRAHAM

Billy Graham is a man of faith. His great faith in God, His redemption, His plan for every life, His love for every person, and the place that God has for him in this day marks him as the leader in the world of religion and the best known living person in the world today. His personal faith and evangelistic fervor have encouraged the multitudes and brought millions to Christ as Saviour and Lord.

God has led him to undertake whatever he does. God has given him the faith to believe that there is a specific purpose in what he does, and that God has specific results which He desires to come from each place he goes. Billy Graham does not trust in any attribute, capacity, or quality of his own, but has an implicit faith in God to do His work through him.

One day in talking with his lovely mother, I asked what she felt was the one quality that enabled Billy to be such an instrument of God and what made it possible for God to do His great work through him. She replied, "I do not know exactly, but I do know this one thing: that when Billy gave his life to God, he gave Him all of it; and he has faith to believe that God has chosen him to be a person through which God can do His work. He has implicit faith."

Billy Graham believes that God has spoken in a very unique way in the Bible and that the Bible is the revealed truth of God. He does not hesitate to emphasize what he believes. And what he believes is from the Bible, God's Holy Word.

In reference to the Bible, Mr. Graham has said that the only real authority we have is God's Word, and the Bible. His Word sheds light on human nature, world problems, and human suffering. But beyond that it delineates and reveals the way back to God.

He has further stated that the Bible is the Constitution of the Christian religion. Just as the United States Constitution is not of any private interpretation, neither is the Bible of any private interpretation. Just as the Constitution includes all who live under its stated domain, without exception, so the Bible includes all who live under its stated domain, without exception.

Billy Graham has great faith concerning the second coming of Christ and what will take place at this blessed event. About this he has said that the Bible accurately predicted Christ's first advent in every detail. Hundreds of years before Jesus was born, the Bible revealed that He would be of the tribe of Judah, that He would be born in Bethlehem, that He would be born of a virgin, that He would flee into Egypt, that He would heal the sick, that His own people would reject Him, that He would be betrayed by a friend and sold for thirty pieces of silver, that He would be crucified with sinners, that His side would be pierced, that He would be raised from the dead and that He would ascend into heaven. And in the same manner Billy believes that the Bible speaks truly of the second coming of Christ.

In this regard, he uses the Bible to teach that the end will come with the coming again of Jesus Christ and that He will set up a kingdom of righteousness and social justice where hatred, greed, and jealousy will no longer be known.

In his emphasis on the Bible he has stated that the Bible is more up-to-date than the morning newspaper.

His faith has enabled him to speak forthrightly on all the issues of the day, but with the reminder that man must be redeemed before the social issues can be corrected.

Billy Graham's faith is that God, alone, has the answer for our world. He sees a basic problem facing our world not that of social inequity, lack of education, or even physical hunger. He has observed that even in the highly educated, well-fed people with their greeds, hate, passion, and lusts, humans' ills are not cured through a process of education. He sees the root of sin in people's hearts as the basic cause of the world's problems and that only the power of the Lord can bring about a change in mankind.

His faith is that God is the Sovereign of the world as it now is. Humankind has defaced it but in His own good time God will bring history to an end. Even science acknowledges that the end of the world, in the near future, is more than a remote possibility.

As this great evangelist proclaims the Word of God, he has a way of pointing his finger and looking people straight in the eye to remind them that sin is a grim fact. It stands like a titanic force, a threat contesting all the good that men may try to accomplish. Sin is akin to a dark shadow ever ready to blot out whatever light may reach us from on high.

Probably more than any evangelist of any generation, Billy Graham has faith in the potentiality of young people and addresses much of his thoughts and messages to them. That young people respond to this is evidenced in the fact that in most of the crusades as much as 75% of the crowd will be 25 years of age and younger. His love for young people has caused him to emphasize his faith in them and his belief that only God has the right answer for them. He is quite frank in discussing with them the problems of sex, and reminds them that it is much better to be moral and pure, and have God in their lives and heaven for their eventual home, than to have the misery and misunderstanding that accompanies the impurities of a worldly life.

In this regard, he has stated that the Bible does not teach that sex is sin. The sex urge, which comes to girls at approximately eleven years of age and a little later for boys, is not a sin. Don't let anyone tell you it's dirty, either. It's not. It's a gift from God. God gave it to people for two reasons: to propagate the race and to provide climax and fulfillment of true love within the bonds of matrimony, but only in the bonds of matrimony.

Mr. Graham is sought after by royalty, presidents, diplomats, business executives, farmers, ditch diggers, labor, the troubled, the great and lowly — of all races, all creeds.

It is because of Billy Graham's great Biblical faith that this book has been published. In it are passages of inspiration and faith from Mr. Graham's sermons—each referring to a specific Scripture. On the opposite page, the Scriptural passage referred to is printed in full, to give the reader a greater insight into sources of The Faith of Billy Graham—and to provide further inspiration for those who hold so dear the words of The Holy Bible and the words of Billy Graham.

Millions of people in every nation of the world pray for this evangelist and also give thanks to God for such a leader in these critical times—Billy Graham—a man of faith.

CORT R. FLINT

The Faith of
BILLY GRAHAM

However, I am convinced that the basic problem of the American home is not the removal of external props but the lack of a deep spiritual commitment to the Lord. It is all right to read the counselor columns in the newspapers and listen to the advisors on radio and TV, but most of them have forgotten that it was God who performed the first marriage in the Garden of Eden and instituted the union between husband and wife. It was God who made the race male and female. It was God who commanded, "Be fruitful and multiply." It was God who said: "It is not good that man should be alone. I will make him a help meet for him." It is God's Word that declares, "Therefore shall a man leave his father and his mother, and shall cleave unto his wife: and they shall be one flesh." When God instituted matrimony, he gave the principles by which a husband and wife are to live.

Ref: GENESIS 2:24

The Arabs and Egyptians are descendants of Ishmael. Ishmael was a son of Abraham of whom the angel of God said centuries ago, "He will be a wild man; his hand will be against every man, and every man's hand against him."

Ref: GENESIS 16:12

The Bible also teaches that life is like a shadow, like a fleeting cloud moving across the face of the sun. The Psalmist says, "We are strangers before thee, and sojourners, as were all our fathers." The world is not a permanent home, it is only temporary. "Our days on the earth are as a shadow, and there is none abiding."

Ref: I CHRONICLES 29:15; PSALM 39:12

GENESIS 2:24

Therefore shall a man leave his father and his mother, and shall cleave unto his wife: and they shall be one flesh.

GENESIS 16:12

And he will be a wild man? his hand will be against every man, and every man's hand against him; and he shall dwell in the presence of all his brethren.

I CHRONICLES 29:15

For we are strangers before thee, and sojourners; as were all our fathers: our days on the earth are as a shadow and there is none abiding.

PSALM 39:12

Hear my prayer, O LORD, and give ear unto my cry; hold not thy peace at my tears: for I am a stranger with thee, and a sojourner, as all my fathers were.

God said: "And thou shalt teach them diligently unto thy children, and shalt talk of them when thou sittest in thine house, and when thou walkest by the way, and when thou liest down, and when thou risest up." In other words, the Bible says that we are to teach our children all day long by precept and example.

If a child is to mature, he must learn to observe rules. Whether we like it or not, life is filled with rules and laws. If a child is to survive, he must know the rules of health. If he is to get along with people, he must learn the rules of etiquette and courtesy. If he is to drive a car, he must learn the rules of the road. If he becomes a ball player, he must learn to observe the rules of the game. Contrary to the thinking of some people, children like rules. They want to know what is expected of them. They like to be guided. It gives them a sense of belonging as well as a sense of security.

Ref: DEUTERONOMY 6:7

The Scriptures teach that back of the world system in which we live is a supernatural satanic power. Job once said, "The earth is given into the hand of the wicked." Jesus, speaking to the sinners of His day said, "Ye do the deeds of your father . . ." "Ye are of your father the devil, and the lusts of your father ye will do . . ."

Jesus called Satan "the prince of this world." The Bible teaches that he is the "god of this world who blinds the mind of them which believe not, lest the light of the glorious gospel of Christ, who is the image of God, should shine unto them."

The Bible teaches that Satan can transform himself into an angel of light and deceive even Christians! Thus, impurity has a better press agent than purity. Satan in selling sex wholesale plays up the momentary thrill, but the consequences of this vicious sin are played down.

Ref: JOB 9:24; JOHN 8:41 and 44

DEUTERONOMY 6:7

And thou shalt teach them diligently unto thy children, and shalt talk of them when thou sittest in thine house, and when thou walkest by the way, and when thou liest down, and when thou risest up.

JOB 9:24

The earth is given unto the hand of the wicked: he covereth the faces of the judges thereof; if not, where, and who is he.

JOHN 8:41

Ye do the deeds of your father. Then said they to him, We be not born of fornication: we have one Father, even God.

JOHN 8:44

Ye are of your father the devil, and the lusts of your father ye will do. He was a murderer from the beginning, and abode not in the truth, because there is no truth in him. When he speaketh a lie, he speaketh of his own: for he is a liar, and the father of it.

When Job could find no human explanation for his agonies, he cried to God, "Show me wherefore thou contendest with me."

This question, "Why must the righteous suffer?" is as old as time. There is only one place that we can find an answer, and that is in the Bible. Yet in their blindness some men have rejected divine guidance and insist that everything in life comes from chance. Fate, they declare, has smiled on the people who have an easy, rich, untroubled existence, and Fate has frowned on those who are beset with unnumbered difficulties. They say that it is a matter of luck. "Since we are only creatures of accident," they conclude, "why not press every drop out of pleasure while we can, and have our full fling before tomorrow comes and death with it?"

Ref: JOB 10:2

The Scripture teaches that God knows the exact moment when each man is to die. There are appointed bounds beyond which we cannot pass. I am convinced that when a man is prepared to die, he is also prepared to live. The primary goal in life therefore should be to prepare for death. Everything else should be secondary.

Ref: JOB 14:5

There are no troubles that distress the mind and wear upon the nerves as do borrowed troubles. The Psalmist said, "Fret not thyself . . ." The implication is that fretting, complaining, and distress of mind are often self-manufactured and can best be coped with by a change of attitude and transformation of thought.

Ref: PSALM 37:1

JOB 10:2

I will say unto God, Do not condemn me; show me wherefore thou contendest with me.

JOB 14:5

Seeing his days are determined, the number of his months are with thee, thou hast appointed his bounds that he cannot pass.

PSALM 37:1

Fret not thyself because of evil doers, neither be thou envious against the workers of iniquity.

You cannot allay a baby's anxiety by giving him a rattle when he is hungry. He will keep on crying until his hunger is satisfied by the food his little body demands. Neither can the soul of a mature person be satisfied apart from God. David described the hunger of all humans when he said: "As the hart panteth after the water brooks, so panteth my soul after thee, O God." The prodigal son, who had to learn life's lessons by painful experience, said: "How many hired servants of my father's have bread enough and to spare, and I perish with hunger!"

Ref: PSALM 42:1; LUKE 15:17

Two conflicting forces cannot exist in one human heart. When doubt reigns, faith cannot abide. Where hatred rules, love is crowded out. Where selfishness rules, there love cannot dwell. When worry is present, trust cannot crowd its way in.

The very best prescription for banishing worry is found in Psalm 37:5: "Commit thy way unto the Lord; trust also in Him; and He shall bring it to pass." The word "commit" means to turn over to, to entrust completely.

Some years ago someone gave my little boy a dollar. He brought it to me and said, "Daddy, keep this for me." But in a few minutes he came back and said, "Daddy, I'd better keep my own dollar." He tucked it in his pocket and went out to play. In a few minutes he came back with tears in his eyes, saying, "Daddy, I lost my dollar. Help me find it." How often we commit our burdens to the Lord and then fail to trust Him by taking matters into our own hands. Then, when we have messed things up, we pray, "Oh, Lord, help me, I'm in trouble."

Ref: PSALM 37:5

PSALM 42:1

As the hart panteth after the water brooks, so panteth my soul after thee, O God.

LUKE 15:17

And when he came to himself, he said, How many hired servants of my father's have bread enough and to spare, and I perish with hunger!

PSALM 37:5

Commit thy way unto the LORD; trust also in him, and he shall bring it to pass.

Many of you who listened to "The Hour of Decision" week by week are bedridden. The Bible says, "The Lord will strengthen him upon the bed of languishing: thou wilt make all his bed in his sickness." God is especially close to us when we are lying on a sickbed; God will make the bed soft and will freshen it with his presence and with his tender care. He makes the bed comfortable and wipes away our tears. He ministers to us with special tenderness at such a time and reveals his great love for us.

Again, the Scripture says, "Fear thou not; for I am with thee: be not dismayed; for I am thy God: I will strengthen thee; yea, I will help thee; yea, I will uphold thee with the right hand of my righteousness."

Ref: PSALM 41:3; ISAIAH 41:10

The simple truth is this—man's heart without God is like a vacuum. In our self-sufficiency we try to make it alone without God. When the going gets rough, however, we need outside help. If we refuse to turn to God who has promised to be a "present help in trouble" we must resort to all sorts of things—pleasure, lust, drunkenness, revelings, and wantonness.

Ref: PSALM 46:1

There is a second sense in which it is later than we think. It is later in our lives than we think. The Scriptures teach that "we spend our years as a tale that is told. The days of our years are threescore years and ten; and if by reason of strength they be fourscore years, yet is their strength labor and sorrow; for it is soon cut off, and we fly away."

James asked, "What is your life? It is even a vapor, that appeareth for a little time, and then vanisheth away."

We have grown familiar with the customary proverbs about the brevity of life, and familiarity often seems to have bred contempt. A sophisticated generation smiles nonchalantly when the minister points out how short is our earthly pilgrimage.

Ref: PSALM 90:9, 10; JAMES 4:14

PSALM 41:3

The LORD will strengthen him upon the bed of languishing: thou wilt make all his bed in his sickness.

ISAIAH 41:10

Fear thou not; for I am with thee: be not dismayed; for I am thy God: I will strengthen thee; yea, I will help thee; yea, I will hold thee with the right hand of my righteousness.

PSALM 46:1

God is our refuge and strength, a very present help in trouble.

PSALM 90:9, 10

For all our days are passed away in thy wrath; we spend our years as a tale that is told.

The days of our years are threescore years and ten; and if by reason of strength they be fourscore years, yet is their strength labour and sorrow: for it is soon cut off, and we fly away.

JAMES 4:14

Whereas ye know not what shall be on the morrow. For what is your life? It is even a vapour, that appeareth for a little time and then vanisheth away.

Does God care for me? The Psalmist voiced the sentiments of many of us when he said: ". . . refuge failed me; no man cared for my soul." Martha, over-concerned with her workaday duties, said to Jesus: "Lord, dost Thou not care?" How many faithful, loving parents, overwhelmed by the burdens of parenthood, have cried anxiously, "Lord, does Thou not care?" The disciples, tossed by the turbulent sea, cried: "Carest Thou not that we perish?"

That question is forever answered in those reassuring words of Peter: "He careth for you." This is the Word of God, and the world will pass away before it can be altered. You can be positively assured that God does care for you, and if God cares for you and has promised to carry your burdens and cares, then nothing should distress you.

Ref: PSALM 142:4

Another basic need of humans is affection. Those who "abide in him" are the objects of God's affection and love. David said, "Because he hath set his love upon me, therefore will I deliver him; I will set him on high because he hath known my name."

Ref: PSALM 91:14

PSALM 142:4

I looked on my right hand, and beheld, but there was no man that would know me; refuge failed me; no man cared for my soul.

PSALM 91:14

Because he hath set his love upon me, therefore will I deliver him. I will set him on high, because he hath known my name.

This brings us to the invitation to live in the realm of God. Jesus said, "Abide in me, and I in you." Personal salvation is not an occasional rendezvous with Deity; it is an actual dwelling with God. Christianity is not just an avocation; it is a lifelong, eternity-long vocation. David, thrilled with the knowledge that his life was in God, said "He that dwelleth in the secret place of the Most High shall abide under the shadow of the Almighty."

If you read and reread this beautiful Psalm, you will discover that in him we have a permanent abode and residence, and that all of the comfort, security and affection which the human heart craves is found in him.

Modern psychiatrists say that one of the basic needs of humans is security. In this Psalm we are assured that in God we have the greatest of security: "There shall no evil befall thee, neither shall any plague come nigh thy dwelling. For he shall give his angels charge over thee, to keep thee in all thy ways."

Ref: PSALM 91:10, 11

Children want their parents to care enough about them to be strict. The Bible teaches us to discipline our children. "He that spareth his rod hateth his son: but he that loveth him chasteneth him betimes."

We owe our children a spiritual training. The Scripture says, "Train up a child in the way he should go: and when he is old, he will not depart from it."

Ref: PROVERBS 13:24 and 22:6

God is concerned with your imaginations, for in a large measure they determine what kind of person you are. Solomon said, "As [a man] thinketh in his heart, so is he." If your thoughts are evil, then your acts will be evil. If your thoughts are godly, then your life will likely be godly. If the wickedness of man at the time of the flood "grieved God at his heart," is it not reasonable to believe that his heart is grieved today by all the sin and lust in the world?

Ref: PROVERBS 23:7

PSALM 91:10, 11

There shall no evil befall thee, neither shall any plague come nigh thy dwelling.

For he shall give his angels charge over thee, to keep thee in all thy ways.

PROVERBS 13:24

He that spareth his rod hateth his son; but he that loveth him chasteneth him betimes.

PROVERBS 22:6

Train up a child in the way he should go; and when he is old, he will not depart from it.

PROVERBS 23:7

For as he thinketh in his heart, so is he: Eat and drink, saith he to thee; but his heart is not with thee.

Remember, the majority of children acquire the characteristics and habits of their parents.

The Bible says, "Train up a child in the way he should go: and when he is old, he will not depart from it." Now some parents carry discipline too far, continually harassing their children. The Bible also says, "Provoke not your children to anger, lest they be discouraged." Parents should never give unreasonable and repetitious commands. Nor should they ever give a command that they do not mean to be carried out.

Ref: PROVERBS 22:6; COLOSSIANS 3:21

The Bible is one of the world's outspoken books on the subject of sex, and the Bible condemns sex outside the bonds of matrimony. The fact that immorality is rampant throughout the nation doesn't make it right; the fact that some clergymen condone it doesn't make it right; The Bible says, "There is a way that seemeth right unto a man; but the end thereof are the ways of death." Under Jewish law adultery was punishable by death. Under God's law today it also results in spiritual death. The Bible says, "She that liveth in pleasure is dead while she liveth." The Bible says, "The wages of sin is death," and, "The soul that sinneth, it shall die."

Ref: PROVERBS 16:25; I TIMOTHY 5:6; ROMANS 6:23; EZEKIEL 18:20

Our crime rate, oddly enough, has increased in exact ratio to our mounting alcoholic consumption. I'm not saying that non-drinking persons do not commit crime, but I am saying that drunkenness preconditions a person for crime and evil, and the facts bear me out. No wonder the Bible says "Wine is a mocker, strong drink is raging: and whosoever is deceived thereby is not wise."

Ref: PROVERBS 20:1

PROVERBS 22:6

Train up a child in the way he should go; and when he is old, he will not depart from it.

COLOSSIANS 3:21

Fathers, provoke not your children to anger, lest they be discouraged.

PROVERBS 16:25

There is a way that seemeth right unto a man; but the end thereof are the ways of death.

I TIMOTHY 5:6

But she that liveth in pleasure is dead while she liveth.

ROMANS 6:23

For the wages of sin is death; but the gift of God is eternal life, through Jesus Christ our Lord.

EZEKIEL 18:20

The soul that sinneth, it shall die. The son shall not bear the iniquity of the father, neither shall the father bear the iniquity of the son; the righteousness of the righteous shall be upon him, and the wickedness of the wicked shall be upon him.

PROVERBS 20:1

Wine is a mocker, strong drink is raging: and whosoever is deceived thereby is not wise.

Many of our news magazines continue to carry stories of immorality. Protestant theologians and pastors are being freely quoted as condoning sexual immorality under certain circumstances. The Bible says through Isaiah the prophet: "Woe unto them that call evil good, and good evil; that put darkness for light, and light for darkness; that put bitter for sweet, and sweet for bitter!"

Ref: ISAIAH 5:20

Yet there is a happiness in the Christian life. Paul said he could be content wherever he was—in jail, in a shipwreck. A hard life? Yes, but a happy one. "Constructive activity," the psychologists tell us, "brings happiness." You will find contentment in following Christ, because it is God's way—and the only way.

You may complain that that is a narrow point of view. You may be on a road that you think is dead right, but God says it is dead wrong. "There is a way which seemeth right unto a man, but the end thereof are the ways of death."

Ref: PROVERBS 14:12

Christ today is big enough to cope with the tyranny of human over human. We have "spiritualized" too much. We have talked about a personal faith in Christ—and that is important. But His power also has world-wide implication. Isaiah said, "The government shall be upon His shoulder." He has not abdicated His sovereignty in the affairs of humans. He is still the Lord of history. When He was crucified, the Bible says, "And a superscription also was written over Him in letters of Greek (the language of culture), and Latin (the language of government), and Hebrew (the language of religion), THIS IS THE KING OF THE JEWS." He was then, and still is, King; but we have failed to acknowledge Him.

One of the ways we have failed is that we have not seen Christ as King of the physical, as well as the spiritual, of the mind as well as the soul.

Ref: ISAIAH 9:6; LUKE 23:38

ISAIAH 5:20

Woe unto them that call evil good, and good evil, that put darkness for light, and light for darkness; that put bitter for sweet, and sweet for bitter!

PROVERBS 14:12

There is a way which seemeth right unto a man, but the end thereof are the ways of death.

ISAIAH 9:6

For unto us a child is born, unto us a son is given, and the government shall be upon his shoulder; and his name shall be called Wonderful, Counsellor, The mighty God, The everlasting Father, The Prince of Peace.

LUKE 23:38

And a superscription also was written over him in letters of Greek, and Latin, and Hebrew, THIS IS THE KING OF THE JEWS.

The Bible is not silent about any force which threatens the souls of humans. It lashes out against any and all of Satan's tricks and devices, and it is very clear in its denunciation of drunkenness.

The Bible says, "Woe to the crown of pride, to the drunkards of Ephraim . . ."

The Bible again says, "Woe unto him that giveth his neighbor drink, that puttest thy bottle to him, and makest him drunken also . . ."

"And take heed to yourselves, lest at any time your hearts be overcharged with surfeiting and drunkenness . . ."

Again the Bible says, "Let us walk honestly, as in the day; not in rioting and drunkenness . . ."

"Woe unto them that rise up early in the morning, that they may follow strong drink; that continue until night . . ."

Again the Bible says, "Be not drunk with wine, wherein is excess . . ."

Ref: ISAIAH 28:1; HABAKKUK 2:15; LUKE 21:34; ROMANS 13:13; ISAIAH 5:11; EPHESIANS 5:18

The Bible teaches that we are to train our children "precept upon precept, line upon line; here a little, and there a little." In other words, you cannot give them religion and morality all at one time. You cannot suddenly wake up, when a boy or girl has reached the age of 12, and say, "It's very late; but I'm going to try to cram religion into him or her now." It must start the very moment he or she has any understanding at all. Precept upon precept, line upon line, it has to be a little here and a little there.

Ref: ISAIAH 28:10

ISAIAH 28:1

Woe to the crown of pride, to the drunkards of Ephraim, whose glorious beauty is a fading flower, which are on the head of the fat valleys of them that are overcome with wine!

HABAKKUK 2:15

Woe unto him that giveth his neighbour drink, that puttest thy bottle to him, and makest him drunken also, that thou mayest look on their nakedness!

LUKE 21:34

And take heed to yourselves, lest at any time your hearts be overcharged with surfeiting, and drunkenness, and cares of this life, and so that day come upon you unawares.

ROMANS 13:13

Let us walk honestly, as in the day; not in rioting and wantonness, not in strife and envying.

ISAIAH 5:11

Woe unto them that rise up early in the morning that they may follow strong drink; that continue until night, till wine inflame them!

EPHESIANS 5:18

And be not drunk with wine, wherein is excess; but be filled with the Spirit.

ISAIAH 28:10

For precept must be upon precept, precept upon precept; line upon line, line upon line; here a little, and there a little.

The Bible further teaches that Christians suffer in order that God might teach them lessons in prayer. Isaiah said, "Lord, in trouble have they visited thee, they poured out a prayer when thy chastening was upon them." Christians call upon God more earnestly when his chastening rod is upon them. They never pray with such seriousness, humbleness, brokenness, fervency and frequency as they do when they are under the mighty hand of God. A sincere Christian never prays so sweetly and humbly as when under the rod. Many Christians have a cold prayer life in the day of prosperity, but let the day of adversity come, and they begin to wrestle with God and become very warm in prayer.

Ref: ISAIAH 26:16

Conversion is so simple that the smallest child can be converted, but it is also so profound that theologians throughout history have pondered the depth of its meaning. God has made the way of salvation so plain that "the wayfaring men, though fools, shall not err therein." No person will ever be barred from the Kingdom of God because he or she did not have the capacity to understand. The rich and the poor, the sophisticated and the simple—all of them can be converted.

Ref: ISAIAH 35:8

ISAIAH 26:16

LORD, in trouble have they visited thee, they poured out a prayer when thy chastening was upon them.

ISAIAH 35:8

And an highway shall be there, and a way, and it shall be called, The way of holiness; the unclean shall not pass over it; but it shall be for those: the wayfaring men, though fools, shall not err therein.

Yes, Christ is the only answer to your problem. If you are a parent, then Christ can help you to rear your children in the fear and nurture and admonition of the Lord. If I were not a Christian I would despair of my children in the moral climate in which we are having to rear them. Get the Scripture and its principles ingrained into their souls—"precept upon precept, line upon line", teach them "here a little" and "there a little" from the Word of God. Get them into the habit of going to church every Sunday, of praying daily, and of saying grace at the table. That will solve 90 per cent of the problems you have with your children. If you are a young person seeking thrills, happiness and joy in some of the questionable avenues of pleasure, I beg of you to come to Jesus Christ.

Ref: ISAIAH 28:13

What are we to do about these past, present, and future worries? The Bible says that we are to cast them upon Him. Our guilty past, our anxious present, and the unknown future are all to be cast upon Christ. All of human's burdens and anxieties are wrapped up in these three words: past, present, and future. For the guilt of the past, God says: "I have redeemed thee." . . . "I have loved thee with an everlasting love." . . . "The blood of Jesus Christ His Son cleanseth us from all sin."

Ref: ISAIAH 44:2; JEREMIAH 31:3; I JOHN 1:7

ISAIAH 28:13

But the word of the LORD was unto them precept upon precept, precept upon precept; line upon line, line upon line; here a little, and there a little; that they might go, and fall backward, and be broken, and snared, and taken.

ISAIAH 44:2

Thus saith the LORD that made thee, and formed thee from the womb, which will help thee; Fear not, O Jacob my servant; and thou Jesu-run, whom I have chosen.

JEREMIAH 31:3

The LORD hath appeared of old unto me, saying, Yea, I have loved thee with an everlasting love; therefore with loving kindness have I drawn thee.

I JOHN 1:7

But if we walk in the light, as he is in the light, we have fellowship one with another, and the blood of Jesus Christ his Son cleanseth us from all sin.

I could not end this message without seeking to impress upon you who have never known Christ that it is later than you think. "Seek ye the Lord while he may be found, call ye upon him while he is near. Let the wicked forsake his way, and the unrighteous man his thoughts: and let him return unto the Lord, and he will have mercy upon him, and to our God, for he will abundantly pardon." There is a clear implication in this passage of Scripture that there will come a time when the Lord may not be found; when he may not be near for salvation.

Ref: ISAIAH 55:6, 7

An ancient prophet, amazed at this fantastic situation, exclaimed, "My people have changed their glory for that which is useless. Be alarmed, O heavens, at this; be shocked, O earth, beyond words: for my people have committed two crimes. They have forsaken me, the fountain of living water, to hew for themselves cisterns, broken cisterns, that can hold no water."

Inasmuch as evil is so pervasive, and even the lustful thought is sin, and since the Devil's master mind is busily engaged in devising methods to imbue the minds of human beings with impure thoughts, a successful remedy must embrace something more far-reaching than good laws and good resolutions.

Ref: JEREMIAH 2:11–13

The Bible says, "The wicked are like the troubled sea, when it cannot rest, whose waters cast up mire and dirt." "In the morning thou shalt say, would God it were even! And at even thou shalt say, would God that it were morning!"

Every day I come in contact with mixed-up, paradoxical people; rich people who are held in the grip of insecurity; intellectual people who have lost their way; strong people who live in the fear of weakness and defeat.

Ref: ISAIAH 57:20; DEUTERONOMY 28:67

ISAIAH 55:6, 7

Seek ye the LORD while he may be found, call ye upon him while he is near.

Let the wicked forsake his way, and the unrighteous man his thoughts: and let him return unto the LORD, and he will have mercy upon him: and to our God, for he will abundantly pardon.

JEREMIAH 2:11–13

Hath a nation changed their gods, which are yet no gods? but my people have changed their glory for that which doth not profit.

Be astonished, O ye heavens, at this, and be horribly afraid, be ye very desolate, saith the LORD.

For my people have committed two evils; they have forsaken me, the fountain of living waters, and hewed them out cisterns, broken cisterns, that can hold no water.

ISAIAH 57:20

But the wicked are like the troubled sea, when it cannot rest, whose waters cast up mire and dirt.

DEUTERONOMY 28:67

In the morning thou shalt say, Would God it were even! and at even thou shalt say, Would God it were morning! for the fear of thine heart wherewith thou shalt fear, and for the sight of thine eyes which thou shalt see.

This day God is speaking to our nation in a thousand ways urging us to repent of our sins and to turn to him before it is too late. But as Jeremiah the prophet said, "They have made their faces harder than a rock; they have refused to return." So there is nothing left but judgment.

Ref: JEREMIAH 5:3

First of all, a Christian should bear his suffering. Jeremiah said, "Woe is me for my hurt! My wound is grievous: but I said, Truly this is a grief, and I must bear it." Sometimes we think that our load is too heavy to bear and that we cannot go on any longer. But God never gives us a heavier load than we are able to bear.

Ref: JEREMIAH 10:19

I have found that the Scriptures have become a flame that has melted away unbelief in the hearts of people and moved them to decide for Christ. The Word has become a hammer breaking up stony hearts and shaping them into the likeness of God. Does not the Scripture say: "I will make my words in thy mouth fire," and "Is not my word like as a fire . . . and like a hammer that breaketh the rock in pieces."

Ref: JEREMIAH 5:14 and 23:29

The fact that chastening is a manifestation of the right kind of parental love is also illustrated by God's attitude toward His children. The Bible says: "For whom the Lord loveth He correcteth, even as a father the son in whom he delighteth."

Ref: JEREMIAH 10:24

JEREMIAH 5:3

O LORD, are not thine eyes upon the truth? thou hast stricken them, but they have not grieved; thou hast consumed them, but they have refused to receive correction: they have made their faces harder than a rock; they have refused to return.

JEREMIAH 10:19

Woe is me for my hurt! my wound is grievous: but I said, Truly this is a grief, and I must bear it.

JEREMIAH 5:14

Wherefore thus saith the LORD God of hosts, Because ye speak this word, behold, I will make my words in thy mouth fire, and this people wood, and it shall devour them.

JEREMIAH 23:29

Is not my word like as a fire? saith the LORD; and like a hammer that breaketh the rock in pieces?

JEREMIAH 10:24

O LORD, correct me, but with judgment; not in thine anger, lest thou bring me to nothing.

As a result of the working of Satan upon the minds of humans, the Scripture states that "The heart is deceitful above all things, and desperately wicked." Our Savior warned His disciples: "Out of the heart proceed evil thoughts, murders, adulteries, fornications, thefts, false witnesses and blasphemy."

It is contrary to reason for a thirsty person to turn from a pure, sparkling mountain stream to quench his thirst, from a stale, putrid cistern—yet that is what the human race does when it rejects God's truth and standards in favor of the Devil's impure philosophies.

Ref: JEREMIAH 17:9; MATTHEW 15:19

When Russia betrayed the freedom loving Hungarian people they were only fulfilling the Biblical analysis of the human heart. The Bible says, "The heart is deceitful and desperately wicked: who can know it?"

Ref: JEREMIAH 17:9

Unless we as a nation repent and turn to God, we are going to suffer a judgment such as no nation has ever endured. The prophet Ezekiel said, "Every heart shall melt, and all hands shall be feeble, and every spirit shall faint, and all knees shall be weak as water: behold (the wrath of God) cometh, and shall be brought to pass, saith the Lord God." The writer of the book of Proverbs quotes God as saying, "I also will laugh at your calamity; I will mock when your fear cometh."

Ref: EZEKIEL 21:7; PROVERBS 1:26

JEREMIAH 17:9

The heart is deceitful above all things, and desperately wicked: who can know it?

MATTHEW 15:19

For out of the heart proceed evil thoughts, murders, adulteries, fornications, thefts, false witness, blasphemies.

JEREMIAH 17:9

The heart is deceitful above all things, and desperately wicked: who can know it?

EZEKIEL 21:7

And it shall be, when they say unto thee, Wherefore sighest thou? that thou shalt answer, For the tidings, because it cometh: and every heart shall melt, and all hands shall be feeble, and every spirit shall faint, and all knees shall be weak as water: behold, it cometh, and shall be brought to pass, saith the Lord GOD.

PROVERBS 1:26

I also will laugh at your calamity; I will mock when your fear cometh.

Never question God's great love. Jeremiah the prophet wrote, "The Lord hath appeared of old unto me, saying, Yea, I have loved thee with an everlasting love: therefore with loving kindness have I drawn thee." Paul speaks of God as one "who is rich in mercy, for his great love wherewith he loved us." It was the love of God that sent Jesus Christ to the cross.

But God's love did not begin at Calvary. Before the morning stars of the pre-Edenic world sang together, before the world was baptized with the first light, before the first blades of tender grass peeped out, God was love.

Ref: JEREMIAH 31:3; EPHESIANS 2:4

The Bible also says that God is a God of love. Jeremiah said, "Yes, I have loved thee with an everlasting love." Malachi said, "I have loved you, saith the Lord."

That answers the greatest question that we could ever ask. I have been asked it a hundred times on university campuses. Who am I? What is the purpose of a man's or woman's existence?

You read Hemingway, Eugene O'Neil, John Paul Sartre, Albert Camus, and other writers. All of them are searching for a meaning and purpose to life and to human existence, but they can't find it. So they say, "Life is meaningless, life has no meaning."

The Bible says God Almighty created the human race for a special purpose. God is love. He wanted some other creatures in the universe like himself, made in his image, little gods who had a will of their own who could return love to Him.

Ref: JEREMIAH 31:3; MALACHI 1:2

JEREMIAH 31:3

The LORD hath appeared of old unto me, saying, Yea, I have loved thee with an everlasting love; therefore with loving kindness have I drawn thee.

EPHESIANS 2:4

But God, who is rich in mercy, for his great love wherewith he loved us.

JEREMIAH 31:3

The LORD hath appeared of old unto me saying, Yea, I have loved thee with an everlasting love; therefore with loving-kindness have I drawn thee.

MALACHI 1:2

I have loved you, saith the LORD: yet ye say, Wherein hast thou loved us? Was not Esau Jacob's brother? saith the LORD: yet I loved Jacob?

Malachi the prophet warned, "Will a man rob God? Yet ye have robbed me. But ye say, Wherein have we robbed thee? In tithes and offerings."

We are so guilty of the sin of covetousness that we actually rob God of that which belongs to Him. Millions may be lost because Christians were too covetous to give that which belongs to God. The Scripture warns, "Woe to him that coveteth . . ."

Ref: MALACHI 3:8; HABAKKUK 2:9

Jesus Christ of Nazareth also used slogans in his ministry.

For example, he said, "Blessed are the poor in spirit: for theirs is the kingdom of heaven." It was one of many slogans that he used to announce his own "great society," which is the Kingdom Society. A society has been defined as "a group living together under the same environment and constituting a homogeneous unit or entity."

Ref: MATTHEW 5:3

According to the Bible, morals are not relative—they are absolute and unchangeable. There is nothing in the Bible that would lead us to believe that God has ever lowered His standards. The Seventh Commandment says, "Thou shalt not commit adultery." This has never been revoked or changed in the slightest degree. In fact, Jesus went further and said, "Ye have heard that it was said by them of old time, Thou shalt not commit adultery; but I say unto you, that whosoever looketh on a woman to lust after her hath committed adultery with her already in his heart."

Ref: MATTHEW 5:27, 28

MALACHI 3:8

Will a man rob God; Yet ye have robbed me. But ye say, Wherein have we robbed thee? In tithes and offerings.

HABAKKUK 2:9

Woe to him that coveteth an evil covetousness to his house, that he may set his nest on high, that he may be delivered from the power of evil!

MATTHEW 5:3

Blessed are the poor in spirit: for theirs is the kingdom of heaven.

MATTHEW 5:27, 28

Ye have heard that it was said by them of old time, Thou shalt not commit adultery:

But I say unto you, That whosoever looketh on a woman to lust after her, hath committed adultery with her already in his heart.

Would you like to "lay up for yourselves treasures in heaven"? Then, Christian, take off your coat of pious indifference, roll up your sleeves of Christian fervor and go to work in the teeming vineyard of souls. Opportunities lie all around you. Your neighbors are without Christ, your children are unsaved, your colleagues in business are waiting to see Jesus in you. I challenge you in Christ's name to become an effective, efficient fisher of men.

"I am interested," you say, "but how may I be a disciple of Christ?" The answer must come from God's Word itself. "If any man will come after me," said Jesus, "let him deny himself, and take up his cross daily and follow me." Before you can follow Jesus in discipleship, the selfish, sinful "self" must be crucified, so that Christ is preeminent in your heart and life.

Ref: MATTHEW 6:20; LUKE 9:23

We were never meant to be crushed under the weight of care. We push the button of faith or pull the lever of trust, and our burden is discharged upon the shoulder of Him who said He would gladly bear it. Cast the anxious present upon Him, for He cares for you—says the Bible. The worries of the future are obliterated by His promises. "Take therefore no thought for the morrow. But seek ye first the kingdom of God and His righteousness; and all these things shall be added unto you." This promise, if we obey it, takes all the peevishness out of life and puts purpose into it. It brings all life into balance, and earth's hours become so joyous that they blend into the glory of eternity. Boredom, fretfulness, and anxiety are lost in the wonder of His wonderful grace.

Ref: MATTHEW 6:34, 33

MATTHEW 6:20

But lay up for yourselves treasures in heaven, where neither moth nor rust doth corrupt, and where thieves do not break through nor steal.

LUKE 9:23

And he said to them all, If any man will come after me, let him deny himself, and take up his cross daily, and follow me.

MATTHEW 6:34

Take therefore no thought for the morrow: for the morrow shall take thought for the things of itself. Sufficient unto the day is the evil thereof.

MATTHEW 6:33

But seek ye first the kingdom of God, and his righteousness; and all these things shall be added unto you.

Jesus used the carefree attitude of the birds to underscore the fact that worrying is unnatural. "Behold the fowls of the air: for they sow not, neither do they reap, nor gather into barns; yet your heavenly Father feedeth them." From this He went on to the lilies of the field. "And why take ye thought for raiment? Consider the lilies of the field, how they grow; they toil not, neither do they spin: And yet I say unto you, That even Solomon in all his glory was not arrayed like one of these."

He did not say that we were not to be industrious, for birds are very industrious. They arise early in the morning and go out to collect the provisions that God has supplied. The flowers flourish and are beautifully clothed, but their roots reach down deep to tap the resources that God has put into the ground for their enrichment.

The birds remind us that food should not be our chief concern, and the lilies show us that worrying over appearance does not make us beautiful. And notice further that He said "The fowls of the air," and "the lilies of the field." Domestic fowls and flowers are protected by human hands, but wild ones are cared for by God Himself.

Ref: MATTHEW 6:26; MATTHEW 6:28, 29

MATTHEW 6:26

Behold the fowls of the air: for they sow not, neither do they reap, nor gather into barns; yet your heavenly Father feedeth them. Are ye not much better than they?

MATTHEW 6:28, 29

And why take ye thought for raiment? Consider the lilies of the field, how they grow; they toil not, neither do they spin;

And yet I say unto you, That even Solomon in all his glory was not arrayed like one of these.

But Jesus Christ, who journeyed from heaven to earth and back to heaven again—who knew the way better than any human who ever lived—said, "Enter ye in at the strait gate; for wide is the gate, and broad is the way, that leadeth to destruction, and many there be which go in thereat; because strait is the gate, and narrow is the way, which leadeth unto life, and few there be that find it."

Jesus was narrow about the way of salvation. He plainly pointed out that there are out two roads in life. One is broad—lacking in faith, convictions and morals. It is the easy, popular, careless way. It is the way of the crowd, the way of the majority, the way of the world. He said, "Many there be which go in thereat." But he pointed out that this road, easy though it is, popular though it may be, heavily traveled though it is, leads to destruction. And in loving, compassionate intolerance he says, "Enter ye in at the strait gate . . . because strait is the gate, and narrow is the way, which leadeth unto life."

Ref: MATTHEW 7:13, 14

God's laws have never been amended. God's prescriptions have never been adulterated. God's directions have never been changed. Old remedies are still prescribed for old sins. Old directions still point to old established destinations. Old laws, which were made for our good, are still in force.

The Bible says, "Enter ye in at the strait gate: for wide is the gate, and broad is the way that leadeth to destruction." But "strait is the gate, and narrow is the way that leadeth to life, and few there be that find it."

Christ is first the life, and then, He is the way. Many have mistakenly thought that if they lived a good life and did the best they could that they would or could earn salvation. This is one of the false signposts along the way. The Bible says, "For by grace are ye saved through faith; and that not of yourselves, it is the gift of God."

Ref: MATTHEW 7:13, 14; EPHESIANS 2:8, 9

MATTHEW 7:13, 14

Enter ye in at the strait gate: for wide is the gate and broad is the way that leadeth to destruction, and many there be which go in thereat:

Because strait is the gate, and narrow is the way, which leadeth unto life: and few there be that find it.

MATTHEW 7:13, 14

Enter ye in at the strait gate: for wide is the gate and broad is the way that leadeth to destruction, and many there be which go in thereat:

Because strait is the gate, and narrow is the way, which leadeth unto life: and few there be that find it.

EPHESIANS 2:8, 9

For by grace are ye saved through faith; and that not of yourselves; it is the gift of God:

Not of works, lest any man should boast.

Read in the New Testament some of the statements that Christ made about this place called hell. "Fear not them which kill the body, but are not able to kill the soul: but rather fear him which is able to destroy both soul and body in hell." "Then shall he say also unto them on the left hand, Depart from me, ye cursed, into everlasting fire, prepared for the devil and his angels."

I have heard some people say that they live by the Sermon on the Mount, and therefore they do not believe in hell. But listen to what Christ had to say in that sermon: "Whosoever shall say [to his brother], Thou fool, shall be in danger of hell fire."

Ref: MATTHEW 10:28, 25:4, 5:22

Christ can change your life. Will you let him? He said, "Strait is the gate, and narrow is the way, which leadeth unto life, and few there be that find it." The crowd is taking the other road—the broad and easy road. It is downhill, with plenty of leisure, plenty of boredom and plenty of noise. But the future is only destruction, judgment, and hell.

Come the narrow way. Receive Christ as your Savior. Let him give you the joy, peace and security which everyone is looking for, and which can be found only in him.

Ref: MATTHEW 7:14

It is significant how much Jesus spoke of money, although He had no personal interest in it. He had become poor that we might through His poverty be rich. He said, "The foxes have holes, and the birds of the air have nests; but the Son of man hath not where to lay his head." He carried no purse. His physical requirements were simple. A meal of corn plucked from the roadside and a mossy stone for a bed in quiet Gethsemane fulfilled His needs. His only garment was a seamless robe. To quench His thirst He would get a drink of cool water from Jacob's well. His taxes were paid by gold taken from a fish's mouth.

Ref: MATTHEW 8:20

MATTHEW 10:28

And fear not them which kill the body, but are not able to kill the soul; but rather fear him which is able to destroy both soul and body in hell.

MATTHEW 25:4

But the wise took oil in their vessels with their lamps.

MATTHEW 5:22

But I say unto you, that whosoever is angry with his brother without a cause, shall be in danger of the judgment: and whosoever shall say to his brother, Raca, shall be in danger of the council: but whosoever shall say, Thou fool, shall be in danger of hell fire.

MATTHEW 7:14

Because strait is the gate, and narrow is the way, which leadeth unto life: and few there be that find it.

MATTHEW 8:20

And Jesus saith unto him, The foxes have holes, and the birds of the air have nests; but the Son of man hath not where to lay his head.

Speaking to unbelievers who denied his first coming, Jesus declared: "When it is evening, ye say, it will be fair weather; for the sky is red. And in the morning, it will be foul weather today; for the sky is red and lowering. O ye hypocrites, ye can discern the face of the sky; but can ye not discern the signs of the times?" Millions were blind as to his first coming and millions more are blind as to his second coming.

Ref: MATTHEW 16:2, 3

The natural question comes to you—What shall I do? Where shall I start? Where do I begin? What is my road back to God? There is only one way back to God. Jesus said, "Except ye be converted, and become as little children, ye shall not enter into the kingdom of heaven." Jesus demanded a conversion. This is how to begin! This is where it starts! You must be converted!

Ref: MATTHEW 18:3

Again and again in the Bible we are graciously invited to enter into personal fellowship with Deity, to be his colleague and associate in bringing redemption to a lost and needy world. Someone has said that the Bible is a book of invitations from God to us, urging us to become his partner in redeeming the world.

The first invitation is an invitation to rest.

Jesus said, "Come unto me, all ye that labor and are heavy laden, and I will give you rest." Since the early dawn of human history when his Eden of bliss became a desert of discord, humans have been creatures of restlessness. Apart from God, a human is a dangerous, inconstant creature. When he or she is bereft of the peace which comes from God through the saving Grace of Christ, he or she becomes a "fish out of water."

A second invitation is to discipleship. "Jesus said unto them, Come ye after me, and I will make you to become fishers of men." We are saved to serve; we are redeemed to reproduce spiritually; we are "fished out of the miry clay" so that we in turn may become fishers of humans.

Ref: MATTHEW 11:28; MARK 1:17

MATTHEW 16:2, 3

He answered and said unto them, When it is evening, ye say, It will be fair weather; for the sky is red.

And in the morning, It will be foul weather to day; for the sky is red and lowering. O ye hypocrites! ye can discern the face of the sky; but can ye not discern the signs of the times?

MATTHEW 18:3

Verily I say unto you, Except ye be converted, and become as little children, ye shall not enter into the kingdom of heaven.

MATTHEW 11:28

Come unto me, all ye that labour and are heavy laden, and I will give you rest.

MARK 1:17

And Jesus said unto them, Come ye after me, and I will make you to become fishers of men.

Jesus underscored the fact that his disciples were to live out-flowingly rather than selfishly. To the rich young ruler he said, "If thou wilt be perfect, go and sell that thou hast, and give to the poor, and thou shalt have treasure in heaven." It wasn't the giving away of his goods that Jesus demanded, particularly, but that he be released from selfishness and its devastating effect on his personality and life.

Ref: MATTHEW 19:21

Jesus was intolerant of selfishness when he said, "For whosoever will save his life shall lose it; and whosoever will lose his life for my sake shall find it." The "life" which Jesus urges us to lose is the selfishness that lives within us, the old nature of sin that is in conflict with God.

So, in your life and in mine, "self" must be crucified and Christ enthroned. He was intolerant of any other way, for He knew that selfishness and the Spirit of God cannot exist together.

Ref: MATTHEW 16:25

You know that the hardest thing for you to give up is your money. It represents your time, your energy, your talents, your total personality conveyed into currency. We usually hold on to it tenaciously, yet it is uncertain in value, and we cannot take it into the next world. The Scripture teaches that we are stewards for a little while of all we earn. If we misuse it, as did the man who buried his talent, it brings upon us the severest judgment of God.

The tithe is clearly taught in the Old Testament; and Jesus said to the scribes and Pharisees regarding the tithe, ". . . These (judgment, mercy and faith) ought ye to have done, and not to leave the other (tithing) undone." God said in the Old Testament, "And all the tithe of the land, whether of the seed of the land, or of the fruit of the tree, is the Lord's; it is holy unto the Lord."

Ref: MATTHEW 23:23; LEVITICUS 27:30

MATTHEW 19:21

Jesus said unto him, If thou wilt be perfect, go and sell that thou hast, and give to the poor, and thou shalt have treasure in heaven; and come and follow me.

MATTHEW 16:25

For whosoever will save his life shall lose it: and whosoever will lose his life for my sake shall find it.

MATTHEW 23:23

Woe unto you, scribes and Pharisees, hypocrites! for ye pay tithe of mint, and anise, and cummin, and have omitted the weightier matters of the law, judgment, mercy and faith: these ought ye to have done, and not to leave the other undone.

LEVITICUS 27:30

And all the tithe of the land, whether of the seed of the land, or of the fruit of the tree, is the LORD'S: it is holy unto the LORD.

When that first atomic bomb was exploded in the deserts of the West in 1945, a scientist saw that mushroom and said, "My God, we have created hell."

The Bible tells us that there is a future world fire. Whether it is to be a literal fire or figurative fire, the Bible is warning us of a day when the judgment of God is going to come on the whole world.

Now let's turn back to the Gospel. "And as he sat upon the mount of Olives . . ." Get the picture now. Here is the mount of Olives right outside Jerusalem. Jesus is sitting down teaching with His disciples explaining to them spiritual things and "as he sat upon the mount of Olives, the disciples came unto Him privately, saying, "Tell us, when shall these things be? and what shall be the sign of Thy coming, and of the end of the world?"

Ref: MATTHEW 24:3

Time after time the Scriptures warn of coming judgment. The Bible states frankly that as the end of the age approaches there will be the same conditions that existed just before the flood. These are described with scriptural terseness and comprehensiveness: "And Jehovah saw that the wickedness of man was great in the earth, and that every imagination of the thoughts of his heart was only evil continually." Our Lord Jesus Christ, in warning of coming judgment, said, "And as were the days of Noah, so shall be the coming of the Son of man. For as in those days which were before the flood they were eating and drinking, marrying and giving in marriage, until the day that Noah entered into the ark, and they knew not until the flood came, and took them all away; so shall be the coming of the Son of man."

Ref: MATTHEW 24:37–39; GENESIS 6:5

MATTHEW 24:3

And as he sat upon the mount of Olives, the disciples came unto him privately, saying, Tell us, when shall these things be? and what shall be the sign of thy coming, and of the end of the world?

MATTHEW 24:37–39

But as the days of Noah were, so shall also the coming of the Son of man be.

For as in the days that were before the flood, they were eating and drinking, marrying and giving in marriage, until the day that Noah entered into the ark.

And knew not, until the flood came, and took them all away: so shall also the coming of the Son of man be.

GENESIS 6:5

And God saw that the wickedness of man was great in the earth, and that every imagination of the thoughts of his heart was only evil continually.

The Bible teaches that the prevalence of knowledge without wisdom is one of the unmistakable "signs of the end" that Jesus talked about.

A second sign of the end of this world system is power without peace. Jesus said, "And ye shall hear of wars and rumors of wars . . . For nation shall rise against nation, and kingdom against kingdom."

Ref: MATTHEW 24:6, 7

Jesus said that "Heaven and earth shall pass away, but my words shall not pass away."

Ref: MATTHEW 24:35

Jesus was intolerant toward hypocrisy. He pronounced more "woes" on the Pharisees than on any other group because they were given to outward piety but inward sham. "Woe unto you, scribes and Pharisees, hypocrites!" he said, "for ye make clean the outside of the cup and of the platter, but within they are full of extortion and excess."

Ref: MATTHEW 23:25

I am not going to take you today to the scientific laboratory, to the classroom of the skeptical philosopher or to the office of the agnostic psychologist. I'm going to take you to an empty tomb in the garden of Joseph of Arimathea. Look at the scene. Mary, Mary Magdalene and Salome have just been here. They came to anoint the body of the crucified Christ. They were startled to find the stone rolled away from the door of the tomb, and the tomb empty. An angel stood at the head of the tomb and said, "Whom do you seek, Jesus of Nazareth?" Then the angel said, "He is not here: for he is risen."

Ref: MATTHEW 28:6

MATTHEW 24:6, 7

And ye shall hear of wars, and rumours of wars: see that ye be not troubled: for all these things must come to pass, but the end is not yet.

For nation shall rise against nation, and kingdom against kingdom; and there shall be famines, and pestilences, and earthquakes, in divers places.

MATTHEW 24:35

Heaven and earth shall pass away, but my words shall not pass away.

MATTHEW 23:25

Woe unto you, scribes and Pharisees, hypocrites! for ye make clean the outside of the cup and of the platter, but within they are full of extortion and excess.

MATTHEW 28:6

He is not here; for he is risen, as he said. Come, see the place where the Lord lay.

The Bible teaches that the end will come with the coming again of Jesus Christ, and that he will set up a kingdom of righteousness and social justice where hatred, greed and jealousy will no longer be known.

Jesus said, "So likewise ye, when ye shall see all these things, know that it is near, even at the doors . . . Then shall the end come."

Jesus talked about the end of the world system and the establishment of a kingdom of righteousness. Christ did not engage in fantasy. He was not given to terror tactics. He was truth and veracity personified. He warned, "When you see certain things coming to pass, you can be assured that the end is very near."

Ref: MATTHEW 24:33, 14

Jesus said, "Be ye also ready: for in such an hour as ye think not the Son of man cometh."

Many fallout shelters are being built to protect your bodies, but what about your souls? Are you ready for the events that lie before the human race?

Dr. Charles Myers, telling about a fire that had destroyed the home of a friend, said, "After all, if life is made up totally of houses and furniture and little keepsakes, it is pretty cheap. These things will be lost to me whether I have a fire or not. Ultimately I will be separated from all of them by death. Though they are lost now, it is not the most tragic thing that could happen. The most tragic thing in life would be the loss of that which is eternal. I am a soul. That soul was made in the image of God and was made for God. The most tragic thing that can happen is that the soul be eternally lost."

Ref: MATTHEW 25:44; I PETER 5:7

MATTHEW 24:33, 14

So likewise ye, when ye shall see all these things, know that it is near, even at the doors.

And this gospel of the kingdom shall be preached in all the world for a witness unto all nations: and then shall the end come.

MATTHEW 25:44

Then shall they also answer him, saying, Lord, when saw we thee an hungered, or athirst, or a stranger, or naked, or sick, or in prison, and did not minister unto thee?

I PETER 5:7

Casting all your care upon him, for he careth for you.

Christ has told us enough for us to know that hell is a place to be shunned. He considered it so awful in its darkness, its separation and its agony that he spoke at length, both to the multitudes and to his disciples, about its terrors. He told people to flee from it, to pluck out an offending eye, if need be. "It is better," he said, "for thee to enter into the kingdom of God with one eye, than having two eyes to be cast into hell fire." Jesus used every descriptive word at his command to warn humans to flee the wrath of God that will fall upon sinners who reject God's plan of salvation.
Ref: MARK 9:47

Many times in the New Testament, terms are used to describe Christ and nearly all of the apostles as being mad, crazy, extreme. The Scripture says, "And when his friends heard of it, they went out to lay hold on him (Jesus): for they said, He is beside himself." Again the Scripture says, "And as he (Paul) thus spake for himself, Festus said with a loud voice, Paul, thou art beside thyself; much learning doth make thee mad."
Ref: MARK 3:21; ACTS 26:24

The owner of a luxurious resort hotel confided in me: "Billy, I have everything a man could have materially. I thought I had it made, but lately I have been fed up with it all. I have always wanted these things, but now that I have them they seem less than I thought they would be. I believe life is more than this." He was right. Jesus said: "A man's life consisteth not in the abundance of things which he possesseth."
Ref: LUKE 12:15

Jesus was intolerant toward selfishness. He said, "If any man will come after me, let him deny himself." Self-centeredness is the basic cause of much of our distress in life. Hypochrondria, a mental disorder which is accompanied by melancholy and depression, is often caused by self-pity and self-centeredness.
Ref: LUKE 9:23

MARK 9:47

And if thine eye offend thee, pluck it out: it is better for thee to enter into the kingdom of God with one eye, than, having two eyes, to be cast into hell fire.

MARK 3:21

And when his friends heard of it, they went out to lay hold on him; for they said, He is beside himself.

ACTS 26:24

And as he thus spake for himself, Festus said with a loud voice, Paul, thou art beside thyself; much learning doth make thee mad.

LUKE 12:15

And he said unto them, Take heed, and beware of covetousness: for a man's life consisteth not in the abundance of the things which he possesseth.

LUKE 9:23

And he said to them all, If any man will come after me, let him deny himself, and take up his cross daily, and follow me.

Jesus said, "Take heed, and beware of covetousness: for a man's life consisteth not in the abundance of the things which he possesseth."

The greatest blessing of giving is not on the financial side of the ledger but on the spiritual side. It gives a sense of being honest with God.

Ref: LUKE 12:15

He once said, "The Spirit of the Lord is upon me, because he hath anointed me to preach the gospel to the poor; he has sent me to heal the broken hearted, to preach deliverance to the captives, and recovering of sight to the blind, to set at liberty them that are bruised." Good news for the poor! Good news for the suffering! Good news for the enslaved! Good news for the blind! Christ can indeed cope with the social problems of the world—he has the capacity; and he gives us that capacity when we come to him and accept him as Savior.

Ref: LUKE 4:18

You cannot say that you are friendless when Christ has said, "Henceforth I call you not servants . . . but I have called you friends." To you who lament the fact that you have been bereft of affection and love in this life, I happily commend Christ. He loved you enough to lay down his life for you. Not only that, but by his atonement upon the cross he purchased the favor of God in your behalf.

Ref: JOHN 15:15

LUKE 12:15

And he said unto them, Take heed, and beware of covetousness: for a man's life consisteth not in the abundance of the things which he possesseth.

LUKE 4:18

The Spirit of the Lord is upon me, because he hath anointed me to preach the gospel to the poor; he hath sent me to heal the broken-hearted, to preach deliverance to the captives, and recovering of sight to the blind, to set at liberty them that are bruised.

JOHN 15:15

Henceforth I call you not servants; for the servant knoweth not what his lord doeth: but I have called you friends: for all things that I have heard of my Father I have made known unto you.

Commit yourself fully to Christ. Don't be a half-surrendered Christian. Among the greatest words that Jesus ever uttered were: "Father, into thy hands I commend my spirit." Even in the heat and conflict of battle his heart, soul, mind and strength were dedicated to the purpose and will of his heavenly Father. The truly happy Christian is the one who is fully and wholeheartedly committed to Christ. Be that kind of follower of Christ!

Ref: LUKE 23:46

Second, we repent of our sins. Jesus said: "Except ye repent, ye shall . . . perish." He said: "Repent . . . and believe. Repentance does not mean simply that we are to be sorry for the past. To be sorry is not enough; we must repent. This means that we must turn our backs on sin.

Third, we receive Jesus Christ as Savior and Lord. "But as many as received him, to them gave he power to become the sons of God, even to them that believe on his name." This means that we accept God's offer of love, mercy and forgiveness. This means that we accept Jesus Christ as our only Lord and only Savior.

Fourth, we confess Christ publicly. Jesus said: "Whosoever therefore shall confess me before men, him will I confess also before my Father which is in heaven." This confession carries with it the idea of a life so lived in front of our fellow humans that they will see a difference. It means also that we acknowledge with our lips the Lord Jesus.

Ref: LUKE 13:3; MARK 1:15; JOHN 1:12; MATTHEW 10:32

LUKE 23:46

And when Jesus had cried with a loud voice, he said, Father, into thy hands I commend my spirit: and having said thus, he gave up the ghost.

LUKE 13:3

I tell you, Nay: but except ye repent, ye shall all likewise perish.

MARK 1:15

And saying, The time is fulfilled, and the kingdom of God is at hand: repent ye, and believe the gospel.

JOHN 1:12

But as many as received him, to them gave he power to become the sons of God, even to them that believe on his name:

MATTHEW 10:32

Whosoever therefore shall confess me before men, him will I confess also before my Father which is in heaven.

You say, "What do you want us to do? I believe in God, I believe in Christ, I believe in the Bible, isn't that enough?" No! By an act of faith you must receive Christ. You must give Him your total life, your intellect, your emotional life. Your will must be bent to His will—surrender, commit, receive. "But as many as received Him to them gave He power to become the sons of God, even to them that believe on His name." Give your life to Him! Don't let anything keep you back! You may never be this close to the Kingdom of God again.

Ref: JOHN 1:12

The same thing that produced juvenile delinquency and crime in America produced the tortuous outburst in Europe. That is the reason Christ said, "Ye must be born again" He knew that it is impossible to create better human relations until humans had been born again of the Spirit of God. Human nature needs redirecting, changing and transforming. There is only one way to make human nature love instead of hate and that is through the regeneration that comes as the Spirit of God transforms the heart that comes to the cross asking for forgiveness and cleansing.

Ref: JOHN 3:7

A third sign mentioned by Christ is religion without saving faith.

Jesus said, "When the Son of man cometh, shall he find faith on the earth?" He also said, "Many shall come in my name, saying, I am Christ; and shall deceive many . . . And because iniquity shall abound, the love of many shall wax cold."

We boast of the revival of religion in America, but we fail to say which religion. It is not a revival of religion in general that will save the world—it is a revival of the belief in the redemptive work of our Lord Jesus Christ.

Christ seems to indicate that toward the end of history there will be a boom in religion. "Many shall come in my name," he said, "and shall deceive many."

Ref: LUKE 18:8; MATTHEW 24:5, 12

JOHN 1:12

But as many as received him, to them gave he power to become the sons of God, even to them that believe on his name.

JOHN 3:7

Marvel not that I said unto thee, Ye must be born again.

LUKE 18:8

I tell you that he will avenge them speedily. Nevertheless, when the Son of man cometh, shall he find faith on the earth?

MATTHEW 24:5, 12

For many shall come in my name, saying, I am Christ; and shall deceive many.

And because iniquity shall abound, the love of many shall wax cold.

Perhaps some of you listening to my voice have broken God's Seventh Commandment. Maybe you have been unfaithful to your wife or husband. Maybe you young people have yielded to sexual immorality. There is hope for you. For all of you who are guilty I have good news. Christ Jesus died upon the cross for you. He shed his blood for you, and the Bible teaches that "the blood of Jesus Christ his Son cleanseth . . . from all sin." Today you can come to the cross and be cleansed of every stain. You can come to the cross and be forgiven of every sin that you have ever committed.

Ref: I JOHN 1:7

We were not made for sin. We were not made for bondage. We were made for life, for joy, for peace, for happiness, for love, for heaven, and for God. Christ is the way. He is the truth. He is the life. "He that believeth not the Son, shall not see life . . ."

Ref: JOHN 3:36

Christ can only do one thing with sin. He does not condone it. He does not condemn it. He forgives it when it is repented.

The Bible says: "For God sent not his Son into the world to condemn the world; but that the world through Him might be saved." When Christ died on the Cross He died for the sin of impurity as for other sins. Actually, impurity is only a symptom of the original sin that David said he was born and shaped in.

Ref: JOHN 3:17

JOHN 1:7

The same came for a witness, to bear witness of the Light, that all men through him might believe.

JOHN 3:36

He that believeth on the Son hath everlasting life: and he that believeth not the Son shall not see life; but the wrath of God abideth on him.

JOHN 3:17

For God sent not his Son into the world to condemn the world; but that the world through him might be saved.

The crowning demonstration and proof of infinite love took place on Golgotha. There God's love for humans was tested in the crucible of suffering as "he gave his only begotten Son, that whosoever believeth in him should not perish, but have everlasting life." The cross expresses the great love of God for humankind; for tradition says that while Christ was hanging there, the angels drew their swords. They announced, "We are going to rescue you." God said, "No," and the Scripture says that God spared him not.

Ref: JOHN 3:16

To the woman taken in adultery in His day, He said, "Thy sins are forgiven thee. Go, and sin no more. He changed Mary Magdalene from a harlot to a woman of purity, whose testimony has thrilled millions through the ages.

To you, man or woman, who have already become guilty of this sin, He can cleanse you and forgive you today, and wipe away every stain—but more. He can give you supernatural power to overcome this temptation. Right now, Christ, through the presence of the Holy Spirit, can give you power to resist those trials and temptations that beset you at this moment. I beg of you, if there is moral sin in your life, that you confess it to Christ, have your sin forgiven, and have Him come into your heart to give you power to face the temptations of tomorrow. Jesus said, "Him that cometh unto Me I will in no wise cast out."

Ref: JOHN 8:11 and 6:37

JOHN 3:16

For God so loved the world, that he gave his only begotten Son, that whosoever believeth in him should not perish, but have everlasting life.

JOHN 8:11 AND 6:37

She said, No man, Lord. And Jesus said unto her, Neither do I condemn thee: go, and sin no more.

All that the Father giveth me shall come to me; and him that cometh to me I will in no wise cast out.

Jesus was intolerant toward sin. He was tolerant toward the sinner but intolerant toward the evil which enslaved him. To Mary Magdalene he said, "Neither do I condemn thee: go, and sin no more." He forgave her because he loved her, but he condemned sin because he hated it with a holy hatred.

God has always been intolerant toward sin! His Word says: "Wash you, make you clean; but away the evil of your doings from before mine eyes; cease to do evil."

"Awake to righteousness, and sin not."

"Let the wicked forsake his way, and the unrighteous man his thoughts . . ."

Christ was so intolerant toward sin that he died on the cross to free us from its power. "For God so loved the world that he gave his only begotten Son, that whosoever believeth in him should not perish, but have everlasting life."

Sin lies at the root of most of society's difficulties today. Whatever separates us from God also separates human from human. The world problem will never be solved until the question of sin is settled.

Ref: JOHN 8:11, 3:16; ISAIAH 1:16, 55:7; I CORINTHIANS 15:34

In the resurrection of Jesus Christ we have the answer to the great question of the ages, "If a human dies, shall he or she live again?" The Bible teaches that because Christ lives, we also shall live. This is the greatest truth of the century, the greatest that your ears can ever hear—that Jesus Christ died but rose again; that we too will die but we can rise again in newness of life to be forever with the Lord.

Ref: JOHN 14:19

JOHN 8:11

She said, No man, Lord. And Jesus said unto her, Neither do I condemn thee: go, and sin no more.

JOHN 3:16

For God so loved the world, that he gave his only begotten Son, that whosoever believeth in him should not perish, but have everlasting life.

ISAIAH 1:16

Wash you, make you clean; put away the evil of your doings from before mine eyes; cease to do evil.

ISAIAH 55:7

Let the wicked forsake his way, and the unrighteous man his thoughts: and let him return unto the LORD, and he will have mercy upon him: and to our God, for he will abundantly pardon.

I CORINTHIANS 15:34

Awake to righteousness, and sin not: for some have not the knowledge of God: I speak this to your shame.

JOHN 14:19

Yet a little while, and the world seeth me no more: but ye see me: because I live, ye shall live also.

To neglect the cross of Christ, to ignore the eternity toward which we are all moving—this is the height of madness. And to disregard salvation through Jesus Christ is the most foolish of all foolishness.

May Christians turn their backs on compromise, easygoing tolerance, and reluctance to be forthright. May we make it clear by word and by action that we really believe that Jesus Christ is "the way, the truth, and the life." Paul's Gospel seemed madness to the world of his day. The Apostle wrote that the Gospel was to the Jews "a stumbling block," and to the Greeks "foolishness." In its reaction to the Gospel, the world of our day has changed little from the world of Paul's day. A true Christian will always be considered queer, strange, unique, mad, and at times even insane.

Let us have this madness! Let us capture some of the magnificent obsession that these early Christians had! Let us go forth as men and women filled with the Spirit of God!

Ref: JOHN 14:6; I CORINTHIANS 1:23

Some time ago I watched a man die, a man who was not a Christian, and it was an experience I shall never forget. I wonder if we are witnessing the death of a nation, death caused by the flouting of God's holy laws, death caused by rejecting God and his Word, death from a social cancer eating at America, death because men and women have turned to their own ways. God has said, "Ye shall die in your sins," but they have listened instead to Satan's siren words: "Ye shall not . . . die."

Ref: JOHN 8:24; GENESIS 3:4

JOHN 14:6

Jesus saith unto him, I am the way, and the truth, and the life: no man cometh unto the Father, but by me.

I CORINTHIANS 1:23

But we preach Christ crucified, unto the Jews a stumblingblock, and unto the Greeks foolishness.

JOHN 8:24

I said therefore unto you, that ye shall die in your sins: for if ye believe not that I am he, ye shall die in your sins.

GENESIS 3:4

And the serpent said unto the woman, Ye shall not surely die.

This invitation to discipleship is the most thrilling ever to come to humankind. Just imagine being a working partner with God in the redemption of the world! Jesus challenged, "If any man serve me, let him follow me; and where I am, there shall also my servant be; if any man serve me, him will my Father honor."

Christian discipleship gives us the privilege of being associated with Christ intimately. And the faithful discharging of the glorious responsibilities of true discipleship invokes the approval and favor of God himself.

Ref: JOHN 12:26

Jesus also said, "If ye continue in my word, then are ye my disciples indeed." A disciple literally means, "a learner, a student, a follower." Salvation may be instantaneous, but discipleship must be learned from the master Teacher, Christ himself. We must know the Word before we can teach the Word. So, the second requirement of discipleship is that we continue in the Word.

Also from the lips of Jesus we hear, "Herein is my Father glorified, that ye bear much fruit: so shall ye be my disciples." If self is slain and the Spirit reigns, the fruits of discipleship are bound to be seen in our lives.

Ref: JOHN 8:31, JOHN 15:8

This brings us to the third invitation, the invitation to live in the realm of God.

Jesus said, "Abide in me, and I in you." Personal salvation is not an occasional rendezvous with Deity; it is an actual dwelling with God. Christianity is not just an avocation; it is a life long, eternity-long vocation. David, thrilled with the knowledge that his life was in God, said, "He that dwelleth in the secret place of the Most High shall abide under the shadow of the Almighty."

Ref: JOHN 15:4; PSALM 91:1

JOHN 12:26

If any man serve me, let him follow me; and where I am, there shall also my servant be: if any man serve me, him with my Father honour.

JOHN 8:31

Then said Jesus to those Jews which believed on him, If ye continue in my word, then are ye my disciples indeed.

JOHN 15:8

Herein is my Father glorified, that ye bear much fruit; so shall ye be my disciples.

JOHN 15:4

Abide in me, and I in you. As the branch cannot bear fruit of itself, except it abide in the vine; no more can ye, except ye abide in me.

PSALM 91:1

He that dwelleth in the secret place of the Most High shall abide under the shadow of the Almighty.

God does not take the Christian out of the world, but He wants His followers to be kept from the love and infatuation of the world's interests and desires, for these temporal things are going to perish. Jesus prayed, "I pray not that thou shouldest take them out of the world, but that thou shouldest keep them from evil."

Paul the Apostle told how the god of this world is blinding people's minds so that they cannot see the glorious gospel of Christ.

John wrote: "Love not the world, neither the things that are in the world. If any man love the world, the love of the Father is not in him. For all that is in the world, the lust of the flesh, and the lust of the eyes, and the pride of life, is not of the Father, but is of the world. And the world passeth away, and the lust thereof: but he that doeth the will of God abideth forever."

Ref: JOHN 17:15; II CORINTHIANS 4:4; I JOHN 2:15–17

This world is not a place of bliss for the Christian, for Jesus reminded us that in this world we would have tribulation; it is part of our earthly inheritance.

Ref: JOHN 16:33

The Bible tells us something of the work of the Holy Spirit. What does He do? We are told that He convicts people of sin, "And when He is come, He will reprove the world of sin, and of righteousness, and of judgment." That's the reason that before you can come to Christ, you must acknowledge that you are a sinner. You must renounce your sins. It is the Holy Spirit that convicts you of your sin. He makes you feel uncomfortable. He pricks your conscience. He makes you acknowledge and admit to yourself that you are a sinner, and then He gives you the strength and the power to turn from your sins.

Ref: JOHN 16:8

JOHN 17:15

I pray not that thou shouldest take them out of the world, but that thou shouldest keep them from the evil.

II CORINTHIANS 4:4

In whom the god of this world hath blinded the minds of them which believe not, lest the light of the glorious gospel of Christ, who is the image of God, should shine unto them.

I JOHN 2:15–17

Love not the world, neither the things that are in the world, If any man love the world, the love of the Father is not in him.

For all that is in the world, the lust of the flesh, and the lust of the eyes, and the pride of life, is not of the Father, but is of the world.

And the world passeth away, and the lust thereof: but he that doeth the will of God abideth for ever.

JOHN 16:33

These things I have spoken unto you, that in me ye might have peace. In the world ye shall have tribulation: but be of good cheer: I have overcome the world.

JOHN 16:8

And when he is come, he will reprove the world of sin, and of righteousness, and of judgment.

Jesus Christ can come in and dominate your life and give you a power to resist evil that you have never known before. Then, and then only, will you find the freedom that you have been searching for. "You shall know the truth, and the truth will set you free." Jesus Christ is the embodiment of all truth, and he will set you free from the power of temptation and the power of evil and sin if you will let him.

Ref: JOHN 8:32

Also from the lips of Jesus we hear, "Herein is my Father glorified, that ye bear much fruit; so shall ye be my disciples." If self is slain and the Spirit reigns, the fruits of discipleship are bound to be seen in our lives.

Ref: JOHN 15:8

To take up the cross means that you take your stand for the Lord Jesus no matter what it costs. It means crucifixion of self — all of your desire for popularity, recognition, success. It may mean that you become the scum of the world. It may mean that you become refuse. It may mean that you become a spectacle to the world. It may mean that you become foolishness to the world. Jesus warned his disciples, "The servant is not greater than his lord. If they have persecuted me, they will also persecute you." As you identify yourself with Christ, you will share in his rejection by the world.

Ref: JOHN 15:20

You cannot say that you are friendless when Christ has said, "Henceforth I call you not servants . . . but I have called you friends." To you who lament the fact that you have been bereft of affection and love in this life, I happily commend Christ. He loved you enough to lay down his life for you.

Ref: JOHN 15:15

JOHN 8:32

And ye shall know the truth, and the truth shall make you free.

JOHN 15:8

Herein is my Father glorified, that ye bear much fruit; so shall ye be my disciples.

JOHN 15:20

Remember the word that I said unto you. The servant is not greater than his lord. If they have persecuted me, they will also persecute you; if they have kept my saying, they will keep yours also.

JOHN 15:15

Henceforth I call you not servants; for the servant knoweth not what his lord doeth: but I have called you friends: for all things that I have heard of my Father I have made known unto you.

Some of the media, including TV, movies, magazines and newspapers, are being criticized for occasional moral degradation. In order to make money, the industry seems to have outdone itself to demonstrate how low the human mind can sink.

The present moral situation reminds us of the burning, seering warnings of the Apostle Paul. He said, "Since they considered themselves too high and mighty to acknowledge God, he allowed them to become the slaves of their degenerate minds, and to perform unmentionable deeds. They became filled with wickedness, rottenness, grand malice: their minds became steeped in envy, murder, quarrelsomeness, deceitfulness and spite. They became whispers-behind-doors, stabbers-in-the-back. God haters; they overflowed with insolent pride and boastfulness, and their minds teemed with diabolical invention. They scoffed at duty to parents; they mocked at learning, recognized no obligations of honor, lost all natural affection, and had no use for mercy. More than this — being well aware of God's pronouncement that all who do these things deserve to die, they not only continued their own practices, but did not hesitate to give their thorough approval to others who did the same."

Ref: ROMANS 1:28–32

Where are we going to turn? The Apostle Paul, many years ago, faced that question from the crew of his storm-tossed ship. He said, "Sirs, ye should have hearkened unto me, and not have loosed from Crete, and to have gained this harm and loss. And now I exhort you to be of good cheer; for there shall be no loss of any man's life among you, but of the ship. For there stood by me this night the angel of God, whose I am, and whom I serve, saying, 'Fear not, Paul; thou must be brought before Caesar: and, lo, God hath given thee all them that sail with thee.' Wherefore, sires, be of good cheer: for I believe God, that it shall be even as it was told me." The angry waves lashed against the ship, the lightning flashed, the thunder roared, yet Paul stood in the midst of the storm and declared, "I have faith in God."

Ref: ACTS 27:21–25

ROMANS 1:28–32

And even as they did not like to retain God in their knowledge, God gave them over to a reprobate mind, to do these things which are not convenient;

Being filled with all unrighteousness, fornication, wickedness, covetousness, maliciousness; full of envy, murder, debate, deceit, malignity, whisperers,

Backbiters, haters of God, despiteful, proud, boasters, inventors of evil things, disobedient to parents,

Without understanding, covenant breakers, without natural affection, implacable, unmerciful:

Who knowing the judgment of God, that they which commit such things are worthy of death, not only do the same, but have pleasure in them that do them.

ACTS 27:21–25

But after long abstinence, Paul stood forth in the midst of them, and said, Sirs, ye should have hearkened unto me, and not have loosed from Crete, and to have gained this harm and loss.

And now I exhort you to be of good cheer: for there shall be no loss of any man's life among you, but of the ship.

For there stood by me this night the angel of God, whose I am, and whom I serve.

Saying, Fear not, Paul; thou must be brought before Caesar; and, lo, God hath given thee all them that sail with thee.

Wherefore, sirs, be of good cheer; for I believe God, that it shall be even as it was told me.

The Apostle John wrote, "I pray . . . that thou mayest prosper and be in health, even as thy soul prospereth." We have failed in some parts of the world because we were afraid to become involved in Christ's program for the total man. Only when Christianity takes on some material as well as spiritual relevance will it be in a position to cope with communism. Liberty, justice and equality are by-products of the Christian faith; and Christ's Golden Rule is at the base of all satisfactory human relations.

Ref: III JOHN 3:2

The responsibility of a husband is to be faithful to his wife. A husband who is unfaithful to his wife in thought, word or deed has committed one of the greatest crimes known to God and man. It is one of the few sins for which God demanded the death penalty in the Old Testament. God says that no adulterer will be found in the Kingdom of Heaven. The wrath of God is waiting at the judgment day for any husband or wife who is unfaithful and guilty of this terrible sin. If you have committed this sin, renounce it, and then confess it to God; the Bible says, "If we confess our sins, he is faithful and just to forgive us our sins." Yes, it is possible for you to be forgiven and cleansed at this moment. It is also possible for you to have victory over the temptations in the days ahead, if you will come in humility and confession to the foot of the cross.

Ref: I JOHN 1:9

III JOHN 3:2

Beloved, I wish above all things that thou mayest prosper and be in health, even as thy soul prospereth.

I JOHN 1:9

If we confess our sins, he is faithful and just to forgive us our sins, and to cleanse us from all unrighteousness.

When the disciples came to Christ and asked of Him saying, "Lord, wilt thou at this time restore again the kingdom of Israel? And He said unto them, 'It is not for you to know the times or the seasons which the Father hath put in His own power. But ye shall receive power, after that the Holy Ghost is come upon you: and ye shall be witnesses unto me . . . unto the uttermost part of the earth.' " In this passage Christ was warning us not to try to predict the exact time of the end of the age and of His coming again. At the same time He was telling us that our job in all circumstances is to be witnesses for Christ.

Ref: ACTS 1:6–8

There are other examples in the New Testament. For example, the infant Christian church made earnest prayer on behalf of Peter, who had been put in prison and was in danger of suffering the fate of the murdered James. Freed by God from jail in answer to their prayers, Peter made his way to the house of Mary, the mother of Mark, where many were gathered to pray. He knocked at the door. Those who were praying were afraid. Rhoda went to investigate, glanced through the hole in the door, and saw Peter standing there. In her excitement she did not let him in but rushed back to tell of his arrival. "You are mad," they said. The news was just too good to be true. "You have worked yourself up into hysteria," they told her. "You've gone crazy." Peter kept knocking at the door, and great was their astonishment when they saw that he really was there!

Ref: ACTS 12:15

ACTS 1:6–8

When they therefore were come together, they asked of him, saying, Lord, wilt thou at this time restore again the kingdom to Israel?

And he said unto them, It is not for you to know the times or the seasons, which the Father hath put in his own power.

But he shall receive power, after that the Holy Ghost is come upon you, and ye shall be witnesses unto me, both in Jerusalem, and in all Judaea, and in Samaria, and unto the uttermost part of the earth.

ACTS 12:15

And they said unto her, Thou art mad. But she constantly affirmed that it was even so. Then said they, It is his angel.

Much so-called worldliness in Christian circles is misunderstood. You cannot confine it to a particular rank, walk or circumstance of life and say that one person is spiritual and another is unspiritual. Worldliness is actually a spirit, an atmosphere, an influence permeating the whole of life and human society, and it needs to be guarded against constantly and strenuously. The Bible admonishes, "Love not the world, neither the things that are in the world." The Bible teaches a life of separation from the evil influences of the world.

Ref: I JOHN 2:15

The Bible teaches that the world as we know it shall end. The Scripture says, "And the world passeth away, and the lust thereof; but he that doeth the will of God abideth for ever." And, "But the day of the Lord will come as a thief in the night; in the which the heavens shall pass away with a great noise, and the elements shall melt with fervent heat, the earth also and the works therein shall be burned up."

Ref: I JOHN 2:17; II PETER 3:10

I JOHN 2:15

Love not the world, neither the things that are in the world. If any man love the world, the love of the Father is not in him.

I JOHN 2:17

And the world passeth away, and the lust thereof: but he that doeth the will of God abideth for ever.

II PETER 3:10

But the day of the Lord will come as a thief in the night; in the which the heavens shall pass away with a great noise, and the elements shall melt with fervent heat; the earth also, and the works that are therein, shall be burned up.

Let me suggest three texts in which we see the three-dimensional sweep of the love of God. In the first one, we see God's love for us: "God commendeth his love toward us, in that, while we were yet sinners, Christ died for us." Penetrating the gloom and despair of this sin-cursed world, even in the dark hours of our present history, is the persistent fact that God loves us.

In our second text, we see the transforming power of love: "We love him because he first loved us." It was Thomas Chalmers who spoke of "the expulsive power of a new affection." When we are possessed of an all-consuming love, it forces all the debris and filthiness out of our hearts.

In our third text, we see a change in our attitude toward others: "When we love God and obey his commands, we love his children too" (NEB). The love principle was the driving force of the first-century church. Its purifying effect kept the stream of early Christianity strong and clean. Peter said, "See that ye love one another with a pure heart fervently."

Ref: ROMANS 5:8; I JOHN 4:19; I PETER 1:22

Christ gives you supernatural power to live the Christian life. You do not struggle alone, by yourself; He lives in your heart to give you power and strength to live the Christian life. You, today, can give your heart to Christ. We read, "Whosoever shall call upon the name of the Lord shall be saved."

Ref: ROMANS 10:13

Again, Scripture teaches that many Christians suffer so that they may have fellowship with others who are in affliction. We read, "Rejoice with them that do rejoice, and weep with them that weep." The Bible teaches us that we are to "bear one another's burdens." Only those who have known sorrow and suffering can have fellowship with those in affliction.

Ref: ROMANS 12:15; GALATIANS 6:2

ROMANS 5:8

But God commendeth his love toward us, in that, while we were yet sinners, Christ died for us.

I JOHN 4:19

We love him, because he first loved us.

I PETER 1:22

Seeing ye have purified your souls in obeying the truth through the Spirit unto unfeigned love of the brethren, see that ye love one another with a pure heart fervently.

ROMANS 10:13

For whosoever shall call upon the name of the Lord shall be saved.

ROMANS 12:15

Rejoice with them that do rejoice, and weep with them that weep.

GALATIANS 6:2

Bear ye one another's burdens, and so fulfill the law of Christ.

Know that Christ lives within everyone of us who has accepted him as Savior. No enemy is too powerful for Christ. Every temptation can be resisted. You can have glorious, daily victory. God said to Joshua, "There shall not any man be able to stand before thee all the days of thy life: as I was with Moses, so I will be with thee: I will not fail thee, nor forsake thee."

The Scripture says: "For sin shall not have dominion over you: For ye are not under the law, but under grace." Paul wrote, "O wretched man that I am! who shall deliver me from the body of this death?" And then he answered his own question: "I thank God through Jesus Christ our Lord."

He further says, "For the law of the Spirit of life in Christ Jesus hath made me free from the law of sin and death." And, "But thanks be to God, which giveth us the victory through our Lord Jesus Christ."

Ref: ROMANS 6:14; I CORINTHIANS 15:57

Drunkenness is related to immorality and sin. "Let us walk honestly . . . not in rioting and drunkenness, not in chambering and wantonness . . .". Drunkenness awakens the passions but puts the soul to sleep. It dulls the reason but sharpens the lustful spirit of humans.

Ref: ROMANS 13:13

The greatest news that mortal ear ever heard was the news that Jesus Christ had risen from the dead as he had promised. The resurrection of Christ is the chief proof of the Christian faith. It is the truth which lies at the very foundation of the Gospel. Other doctrines may be important, but the resurrection is essential. Without a belief in the resurrection there can be no personal salvation. The Bible says if we confess with our mouths the Lord Jesus and believe in our hearts that God raised him from the dead, we shall be saved.

Ref: ROMANS 10:9, 10

ROMANS 6:14

For sin shall not have dominion over you: for ye are not under the law, but under grace.

I CORINTHIANS 15:57

But thanks be to God, which giveth us the victory through our Lord Jesus Christ.

ROMANS 13:13

Let us walk honestly, as in the day; not in rioting and drunkenness, not in chambering and wantonness, not in strife and envying.

ROMANS 10:9, 10

That if thou shalt confess with thy mouth the Lord Jesus, and shalt believe in thine heart that God hath raised him from the dead, thou shalt be saved.

For with the heart man believeth unto righteousness; and with the mouth confession is made unto salvation.

Is America doomed? Is the West doomed? Are we heading for the judgment of a holy God? Have we turned from the God of our fathers to the gods of lust and greed? It is later in this country than we care to think. We have become tolerant of evil to the point of exchanging good for it. We have confused liberty with license, freedom for the bondage of self-indulgence, and the personal opinions of humans for the clearly stated revelation of God. Professing ourselves to be wise, we are becoming fools in God's sight.

Ref: ROMANS 1:22

The law of Moses is set forth in specific terms in the Bible, and the purpose of the law is made very clear. It was not offered at any time as a panacea for the world's ills; it outlines the reason for our trouble, not the cure. The Bible says, "Now we know that what things soever the law saith, it saith to them who are under the law: that every mouth may be stopped, and all the world may become guilty before God." The law has given a revelation of man's unrighteousness, and the Bible says, "By the deeds of the law there shall no flesh be justified in his sight." It is impossible to be converted by the keeping of the law. The Bible says, "By the law is the knowledge of sin."

Ref: ROMANS 3:19, 20

Considering, then, that it is later in the age and later in life than we think, how circumspectly ought Christians to walk, "redeeming the time, because the days are evil." Certainly "the night is far spent, the day is at hand: let us therefore cast off the works of darkness, and let us put on the armor of light. Let us walk honestly, as in the day, not in rioting and drunkenness, not in chambering and wantonness, not in strife and envying. But put ye on the Lord Jesus Christ, and make not provision for the flesh, to fulfill the lusts thereof."

Ref: ROMANS 13:12–14

ROMANS 1:22

Professing themselves to be wise, they became fools.

ROMANS 3:19, 20

Now we know, that what things soever the law saith, it saith to them who are under the law; that every mouth may be stopped, and all the world may become guilty before God.

Therefore by the deeds of the law there shall no flesh be justified in his sight: for by the law is the knowledge of sin.

ROMANS 13:12–14

The night is far spent, the day is at hand: let us therefore cast off the works of darkness, and let us put on the armour of light.

Let us walk honestly, as in the day: not in rioting and drunkenness, not in chambering and wantonness, not in strife and envying.

But put ye on the Lord Jesus Christ, and make not provision for the flesh, to fulfill the lusts thereof.

But the Bible, which has withstood the ravages of time, tells us a different story. It says that we are possessed of a nature that wars against us, that seeks to destroy us. Saul of Tarsus said "I find (in me) a law that, when I would do good, evil is present with me." Evil is present to cleverly disguise itself as good. Evil is present to control us. Evil is present to deceive us. That is what the cross of Christ is all about. That is what the atonement was for, to make us one with him—dead to sin and alive to righteousness.

Ref: ROMANS 7:21

Throughout the behavior of parents, teachers, and teenagers alike there seems to run the theme of freedom from responsibility, which leads directly to rebellion. However, the blame goes far beyond parents and teachers, even beyond the society in which teenagers are reared. The Bible says, "All have sinned," and that includes young people as well as adults. Hundreds of you young people have catered to yourselves. You have made your own rules, and you must share in the responsibility to overcome your rebellion.

Ref: ROMANS 3:23

When Peter declared that in Christ we have one who will dissolve our anxieties and share our burdens, he underlined the truth that "as in Adam all die, even so in Christ shall all be made alive." Christ, being human as well as God, could by his redemptive work on the cross mend the broken partnership between God and man, and he did just that. For all who have been born again by accepting this finished work of Christ, God once again walks with them, talks with them, shares their anxieties and burdens, and lifts the load of care from their weary shoulders.

Ref: I CORINTHIANS 15:22

ROMANS 7:21

I find then a law, that, when I would do good, evil is present with me.

ROMANS 3:23

For all have sinned, and come short of the glory of God.

I CORINTHIANS 15:22

For as in Adam all die, even so in Christ shall all be made alive.

Ask the incurables in our hospitals and sanatoriums who are paying physically for breaking the seventh commandment, if sin brings happiness. As they watch the sands of time run out and as the folly of their youth takes its toll, their voices say eloquently, ". . . the wages of sin is death."

But the sin of impurity at the outset does not appear ugly and venomous. It comes in the guise of beauty, symmetry and desirability. There's nothing repulsive about it.

Ref: ROMANS 6:23

The Apostle Peter wrote, "As newborn babes, desire the sincere milk of the word, that ye may grow thereby." The Apostle Paul commended Christians at Thessalonica, "Your faith groweth exceedingly." Is this your happy experience? Are you full of joy because you are filled with Christ? In seeking to answer that question for you I would suggest this:

First, recognize that temptation is a normal experience. The Bible says that temptation has not taken you in any way that is not common to humanity. In general, it is a part of our ordinary human experience. Christ, as the only perfect human, was, in every respect tempted as we are. Moreover, he felt deeply the spiritual and mental anguish that temptation occasions, for it is written that "He himself hath suffered being tempted."

Ref: I CORINTHIANS 10:13; HEBREWS 4:15 and 2:18

When Peter declared that in Christ we have one who will dissolve our anxieties and share our burdens, he underlined the truth that "as in Adam all die, even so in Christ shall all be made alive."

Ref: I CORINTHIANS 15:22

ROMANS 6:23

For the wages of sin is death; but the gift of God is eternal life, through Jesus Christ our Lord.

I CORINTHIANS 10:13

There hath no temptation taken you but such as is common to man: but God is Faithful, who will not suffer you to be tempted above that ye are able; but will with the temptation also make a way to escape, that ye may be able to bear it.

HEBREWS 4:15

For we have not an high priest which cannot be touched with the feeling of our infirmities; but was in all points tempted like as we are, yet without sin.

HEBREWS 2:18

For in that he himself hath suffered being tempted, he is able to succour them that are tempted.

I CORINTHIANS 15:22

For as in Adam all die, even so in Christ shall all be made alive.

There is a group called carnal Christians. Paul says, "I could not speak unto you as unto spiritual, but as unto carnal, even as unto babes in Christ." A carnal Christian is a person who continually grieves the Holy Spirit by his or her temper, touchiness, irritability, prayerlessness or love of self-esteem. He or she is living a worldly life, not faithful to the church. These are signs of carnality, of spiritual babyhood.

Ref: I CORINTHIANS 3:1

The Apostle Paul wrote, ". . . the blessed and only Potentate, the Kings of kings, and Lord of lords; who only hath immortality, dwelling in the light which no man can approach unto; whom no man hath seen, nor can see: to whom be honor and power everlasting."

No, God is not dead. He is alive forevermore. He is the God of glory in whom we can have confidence and put our trust. Yes, there are those who say God is dead; they say that our Gospel is foolishness. This is precisely what the Apostle Paul said two thousand years ago. He said, "For the preaching of the cross is to them that perish, foolishness; but unto us which are saved, it is the power of God. For it is written, I will destroy the wisdom of the wise, and will bring to nothing the understanding of the prudent. Where is the wise? where is the scribe? where is the disputer of this world? hath not God made foolish the wisdom of this world? . . . Because the foolishness of God is wiser than men; and the weakness of God is stronger than men."

Ref: I CORINTHIANS 1:18–20, 25

I CORINTHIANS 3:1

And I, brethren, could not speak unto you as unto spiritual, but as unto carnal, even as unto babes in Christ.

I CORINTHIANS 1:18–20

For the preaching of the cross is to them that perish foolishness; but unto us which are saved it is the power of God.

For it is written, I will destroy the wisdom of the wise, and will bring to nothing the understanding of the prudent.

Where is the wise? where is the scribe? where is the disputer of this world? hath not God made foolish the wisdom of this world?

I CORINTHIANS 1:25

Because the foolishness of God is wiser than men; and the weakness of God is stronger than men.

To find love defined in sheer poetry, Paul tells us of "a more excellent way," of a path that transcends every other. Rising on wings of inspired utterance, he pours forth his glorious psalm of Christian love, mounting higher and higher in a grand crescendo. He climaxes his classic hymn with these words: "But now abideth faith, hope, love, these three; and the greatest of these is love." Like a prism reflecting the rays of the sun in all the colors of the rainbow, the light of inspiration shines through the pages of the Scriptures, revealing the full-orbed beauty of God's love.

Ref: I CORINTHIANS 13:13

But you say, "We're young, and we have this tremendous energy and power within us. What are we going to do with it?" "Ah," you say, "but I can't resist temptation." Yes, you can! God will never allow you to be tempted beyond your ability to resist the temptation. He will make a way of escape for you. If Christ lives in your heart, you don't have to yield to any temptation. If you are not a Christian, of course, your resistance is in jeopardy. You may have some respectability, some moral principles, but they soon waver and sag, and you give way. But for the true believer in the Lord Jesus Christ there is a way to escape. The Holy Spirit makes that way.

Ref: I CORINTHIANS 10:13

A person without God is a contradiction, a paradox, a monstrosity. He sees evil as good and good as evil. That is why some people love evil and hate that which is good—they are still in their sins. For them, life's values are confused. Paul found the cure for his violent, destructive disposition, not at the feet of Gamaliel or in the culture of Greece, but on the Damascus road when he met Jesus Christ. Later he wrote, "For the law of the Spirit of life in Christ Jesus hath made me free from the law of sin and death."

Ref: ROMANS 8:2

I CORINTHIANS 13:13

And now abideth faith, hope, charity, these three; but the greatest of these is charity.

I CORINTHIANS 10:13

There hath no temptation taken you but such as is common to man: but God is faithful, who will not suffer you to be tempted above that ye are able; but will with the temptation also make a way to escape, that ye may be able to bear it.

ROMANS 8:2

For the law of the Spirit of life in Christ Jesus hath made me free from the law of sin and death.

Yet the whole climate of our daily lives and environment consists of influences which tend to deny any need for a clear-cut separation between the Christian and the world. Many people say, "We mustn't be old Puritans or strait-laced Victorians." Others say, "When you are in Rome, do as the Romans do."

Yet we read in the Word of God such astounding statements as: "Come out from among them and be ye separate, and touch not the unclean thing." So the Christian youth faces a dilemma — which voice will she or he listen to? Which appeal will she or he yield to?

Ref: II CORINTHIANS 6:17

Immorality can be committed by the tongue. The Bible warns about evil communications that corrupt good manners. The Psalmist said, "Set a watch, O Lord, before my mouth." Off-color jokes and dirty stories have no place in the Christian life. Thousands of persons are committing immorality by the way they talk. There are many ways that this can be done, and all the way through the Bible it is condemned as a heinous and grievous sin before God. Yet today millions of persons deliberately disregard the law of God, and the attitude of the church is partly to blame. We fail to teach that God is going to judge this sin.

Ref: I CORINTHIANS 15:33; PSALM 141:3

Three thousand years ago when King Jehoshaphat ascended to the throne of David, his country, like ours, was surrounded by threatening foes. Earnestly and sincerely King Jehoshaphat sought peace for his people as we are doing today. This great ruler was a man of God. The Bible says that "he walked in the . . . ways of his father David" and that he "sought . . . the Lord . . . and walked in his commandments. His heart was lifted up in the ways of the Lord."

Ref: II CHRONICLES 17:3, 4, 6

II CORINTHIANS 6:17

Wherefore come out from among them, and be ye separate, saith the Lord, and touch not the unclean thing; and I will receive you.

I CORINTHIANS 15:33

Be not deceived: evil communications corrupt good manners.

PSALM 141:3

Set a watch, O LORD, before my mouth: keep the door of my lips.

II CHRONICLES 17:3, 4, 6

And the LORD was with Jehoshaphat, because he walked in the first ways of his father David, and sought not unto Baalim:

But sought to the LORD God of his father, and walked in his commandments, and not after the doings of Israel.

And his heart was lifted up in the ways of the LORD: moreover, he took away the high places and groves out of Judah.

First, there is the natural human. The Bible says, "The natural man receiveth not the things of the Spirit of God: for they are foolishness unto him: neither can he know them, because they are spiritually discerned." The Bible teaches us that every person born into the world is born in sin and by nature a child of wrath. We are all separated from God and in ourselves utterly helpless, even though this natural human often puts up a religious front and endeavors by his own effort to please God.

Ref: I CORINTHIANS 2:14

The Bible always links sin and death. You seldom find one mentioned without the other. The Bible says that "the sting of death is sin," that "sin came into the world through one man and death through sin, and so death spread to all men because all men sinned."

Ref: I CORINTHIANS 15:56; ROMANS 5:12

"What's in it for me?" In a world founded on materialism such a reaction is natural and normal.

But in the Kingdom Society not self-interest, but selflessness, is basic. The founder, Jesus Christ, was rich, and yet he became poor that we "through his poverty might be rich." His disciples followed him, and it was said of them, "Neither said any of them that ought of the things which he possessed was his own." Peter, rich in heavenly goods but poor in worldly possessions, said to the lame man on the Temple steps, "Silver and gold have I none; but such as I have give I thee."

The apostles held worldly goods in contempt and cherished the abiding values of the Spirit. They lived with eternity in view. They put service to God and mankind above self-interest. Jesus said, "Greater love hath no man than this, that a man lay down his life for his friends."

Ref: II CORINTHIANS 8:9; ACTS 4:32; 3:6; JOHN 15:13

I CORINTHIANS 2:14

But the natural man receiveth not the things of the Spirit of God: for they are foolishness unto him: neither can he know them, because they are spiritually discerned.

I CORINTHIANS 15:56

The sting of death is sin: and the strength of sin is the law.

ROMANS 5:12

Wherefore, as by one man sin entered into the world, and death by sin; and so death passed upon all men, for that all have sinned.

II CORINTHIANS 8:9

For ye know the grace of our Lord Jesus Christ that though he was rich, yet for your sakes he became poor, that ye through his poverty might be rich.

ACTS 4:32

And the multitude of them that believed were of one heart and of one soul: neither said any of them that ought of the things which he possessed was his own; but they had all things common.

ACTS 3:6

Then Peter said, Silver and gold have I none; but such as I have give I thee; In the name of Jesus Christ of Nazareth, rise up and walk.

JOHN 15:13

Greater love hath no man than this, that a man lay down his life for his friends.

"The fruit of the Spirit is love, joy, peace, long-suffering, gentleness, goodness, faith, meekness, temperance: against such there is no law. And they that are Christ's have crucified the flesh with the affections and lusts. If we live in the Spirit, let us also walk in the Spirit. Let us not be desirous of vain glory, provoking one another, envying one another."

I believe it is impossible to understand the Bible, the structure of the church or Christian living without understanding something of the person and the work of the Holy Spirit.

Ref: GALATIANS 5:22–24

A true disciple of Christ will bear the fruit of the Spirit, which is "love, joy, peace, long-suffering, gentleness, goodness, faith, meekness, and temperance." These fruits are produced in our lives by the Holy Spirit. As we daily yield our wills to him, he produces this supernatural fruit in our lives. People who contact us daily will take note that we have been with Jesus. We will literally radiate Christ. The secret of the Christian life is Christ in us producing fruit.

Ref: GALATIANS 5:22, 23

The Bible says, "God is not mocked: for whatsoever a man soweth that shall he also reap." The Bible also says, "They have sown the wind, and they shall reap the whirlwind." Millions of persons are suffering today because of their sins, iniquities and wickedness. They will not only suffer in this life, but they will suffer throughout eternity unless they repent and turn to Christ as Savior.

Ref: GALATIANS 6:7; HOSEA 8:7

GALATIANS 5:22–24

But the fruit of the Spirit is love, joy, peace, long-suffering, gentleness, goodness, faith,

Meekness, temperance: against such there is no law.

And they that are Christ's have crucified the flesh with the affections and lusts.

GALATIANS 5:22, 23

But the fruit of the Spirit is love, joy, peace, long-suffering, gentleness, goodness, faith,

Meekness, temperance: against such there is no law.

GALATIANS 6:7

Be not deceived; God is not mocked: for whatsoever a man soweth, that shall he also reap.

HOSEA 8:7

For they shall have sown the wind and they shall reap the whirlwind: it hath no stalk: the bud shall yield no meal: if so be it yield, the strangers shall swallow it up.

The Scriptures also have much to say about the motive in giving. The Apostle Paul said, "Every man according as he purposeth in his heart, so let him give; not grudgingly, or of necessity: for God loveth a cheerful giver." We are to give cheerfully and gratefully to the work of the Lord.

Ref: II CORINTHIANS 9:7

The Bible teaches Christ is the head of the church. The Bible uses the wonderful analogy of Christ and the church to describe what the relationship is between husband and wife.

A husband and wife are equal in mind, conscience, position, privilege, freedom and happiness. The Bible says, "The twain shall be one flesh." There is equality before God. There is a balance of power in the home between the husband and the wife.

Ref: COLOSSIANS 3:18

The Bible teaches us that we should be content in suffering. Paul said, "For I have learned, in whatsoever state I am, therewith to be content."

Ref: PHILIPPIANS 4:11

A true disciple of Christ will bear the fruit of the Spirit, which is "love, joy, peace, long-suffering, gentleness, goodness, faith, meekness, and temperance." These fruits are produced in our lives by the Holy Spirit. As we daily yield our wills to him, he produces this supernatural fruit in our lives. People who contact us daily will take note that we have been with Jesus. We will literally radiate Christ. The secret of the Christian life is Christ in us producing fruit.

Ref: GALATIANS 5:22, 23

II CORINTHIANS 9:7

Every man according as he purposeth in his heart, so let him give; not grudgingly or of necessity: for God loveth a cheerful giver.

COLOSSIANS 3:18

Wives, submit yourselves unto your own husbands, as it is fit in the Lord.

PHILIPPIANS 4:11

Not that I speak in respect of want: for I have learned, in whatsoever state I am, therewith to be content.

GALATIANS 5:22, 23

But the fruit of the Spirit is love, joy, peace, long-suffering, gentleness, goodness, faith.

Meekness, temperance: against such there is no law.

Our greatest need is to experience conversion and the new birth. Only this regeneration by the Holy Spirit, which makes a person into a new creature can bring complete protection against the immorality portrayed and practiced all about us. The Bible states our great need in these words: "Put off your old nature, which belongs to your former manner of life and is corrupt through deceitful lusts, and be renewed in the spirit of your minds, and put on the new nature, created after the likeness of God in true righteousness and holiness."

We have an obligation to take steps to reduce the temptation of immorality for the protection of our young people.

Ref: EPHESIANS 4:22–24

Discipline your children. The devil's philosophy is: Do as you please. Children are going to be in society what they are in the home. The Bible, from Genesis to Revelation, teaches that parents ought to discipline their children. "Ye fathers . . . bring them up in the nurture and admonition of the Lord." . . . "He that spareth his rod hateth his son: but he that loveth him chasteneth him." And, "Chasten thy son while there is hope, and let not thy soul spare for his crying."

Ref: EPHESIANS 6:4; PROVERBS 13:24, 19:18

"Set thine house in order," said the prophet. Take the time, trouble and effort to maintain an orderly, disciplined household. The Word of God praises the one who rules his or her own house, "having his children in subjection with all gravity."

Ref: I TIMOTHY 3:4

EPHESIANS 4:22–24

That ye put off, concerning the former conversation, the old man, which is corrupt according to the deceitful lusts;

And be renewed in the spirit of your mind;

And that ye put on the new man, which after God is created in righteousness and true holiness.

EPHESIANS 6:4

And, ye fathers, provoke not your children to wrath: but bring them up in the nurture and admonition of the Lord.

PROVERBS 13:24

He that spareth his rod hateth his son; but he that loveth him chasteneth him betimes.

PROVERBS 19:18

Chasten thy son while there is hope, and let not thy soul spare for his crying.

I TIMOTHY 3:4

One that ruleth well his own house, having his children in subjection with all gravity.

Let us consider the duty of a husband in the home. Husband is an Anglo-Saxon word which means "the band of the house." Just as all our duties to God and humanity are summed up in the word "love," so all the duties which the husband owes the wife are summed up in the command, "Love your wife."

The Scripture says "Let every one of you in particular so love his wife even as himself." Husbands, your first duty, then, is to love your wife. That love should be just as real and genuine after you have been married 25 or 50 years as it was on the day of your wedding. Your love may be less demonstrative, because age is less demonstrative than youth, but it should be just as genuine, manifesting itself in courtesy, politeness, and a loving gentleness toward the woman who has walked by your side these many years.

Ref: EPHESIANS 5:33

Consciously or unconsciously the entire country is engaged at this hour in a mighty, tremendous spiritual warfare. The Bible warns that there will come a time when the very elect—that means the Christians themselves—will be deceived. In other words, there will be a time when the Christian church itself will be deceived by the clever manipulations of Satan. Therefore the Scripture urges us to "put on the whole armor of God, that [we] may be able to stand against the wiles of the devil. For we wrestle not against flesh and blood, but against principalities, against powers, against the rulers of the darkness of this world, against spiritual wickedness in high places."

Ref: EPHESIANS 6:11, 12

EPHESIANS 5:33

Nevertheless, let every one of you in particular, so love his wife even as himself; and the wife see that she reverence her husband.

EPHESIANS 6:11, 12

Put on the whole armour of God, that ye may be able to stand against the wiles of the devil.

For we wrestle not against flesh and blood, but against principalities, against powers, against the rulers of the darkness of this world, against spiritual wickedness in high places.

The Bible has warned: "Whosoever shall keep the whole law, and yet stumble in one point, the same has become guilty of all." In other words, the Bible says you may keep all the Ten Commandments, and yet break the Seventh Commandment in spirit, and you are condemned. Yet, we do not find within ourselves an ability to keep this law, but knowing our inability through sin, God has graciously made provision for all our need, great as it is.

While we are in ourselves unable to live up to the law, and while in our weakened condition through sin we can only acknowledge its truth, yet there is forever mercy with the Lord. To the desperate soul fully aware of all his or her sin and failure, there comes the joyful assurance, "I thank God, through Jesus Christ, our Lord; there is therefore now no judgment to them that are in Christ." Yes, Christ is our hope! His blood on the cross can cleanse from all sin and stain.

Ref: JAMES 2:10; ROMANS 8:1

The Bible says: "Jesus Christ the same yesterday, and today, and for ever." He is the Savior of our yesterdays, forgiving and absolving our guilty past. He is the Christ of today, sharing our griefs and bearing our burdens. He is the Christ of the future, our Alpha and Omega, our joyous beginning and our glorious crowning.

Ref: HEBREWS 13:8

That is why, to begin with, the Bible cautions every person who intends to marry, "Be not unequally yoked together with unbelievers." There is a good reason for this stern command. Marriage is the only abiding relationship in this life. A person may join almost any organization and resign with the full approval of God, but the marriage bond must not be broken.

Ref: II CORINTHIANS 6:14

JAMES 2:10

For whosoever shall keep the whole law, and yet offend in one point, he is guilty of all.

ROMANS 8:1

There is, therefore, now no condemnation to them which are in Christ Jesus, who walk not after the flesh, but after the Spirit.

HEBREWS 13:8

Jesus Christ the same yesterday, and to day, and for ever.

II CORINTHIANS 6:14

Be ye not unequally yoked together with unbelievers: for what fellowship hath righteousness with unrighteousness? and what communion hath light with darkness?

P aul the apostle warned that many will follow these false teachers, not knowing that in gulping down and feeding upon what they say they are taking the devil's poison into their own lives. Thousands of uninstructed Christians are being deceived. False teachers use high-sounding words that seem like the epitome of scholarship and culture. They are intellectually clever and crafty in their sophistry. They are adept in beguiling thoughtless and untaught men and women. Of these people the Apostle Paul said, "Now the Spirit speaketh expressly, that in the latter times some shall depart from the faith, giving heed to seducing spirits, and doctrines of devils; speaking lies in hypocrisy . . .".

Ref: I TIMOTHY 4:1, 2

T he Bible teaches that faith is the only approach that we have to God. "For he that cometh to God must believe that he is, and that he is a rewarder of them that diligently seek him." Faith pleases God more than anything else. "But without faith it is impossible to please him."

Ref: HEBREWS 11:6

I TIMOTHY 4:1, 2

Now the Spirit speaketh expressly, that in the latter times some shall depart from the faith, giving heed to seducing spirits, and doctrines of devils:

Speaking lies in hypocrisy; having their conscience seared with a hot iron.

HEBREWS 11:6

But without faith it is impossible to please him: for he that cometh to God must believe that he is, and that he is a rewarder of them that diligently seek him.

Impurity mocks and deceives. Paul writing to Titus, indicates that he knew the deceitfulness of immorality before he came to know Jesus Christ. He said, "For we ourselves also were sometimes foolish, disobedient, deceived, serving divers lusts and pleasures . . ." This sin has deceived kings, prophets, sages, saints and even preachers. Do not think for one moment that you are immune to its blight.

Even the wise Solomon, who through experience had every reason to know, said, "Fools make a mock at sin . . ."

Too many people underestimate the power of impurity. Samson toyed with it, made sport of it and thought he had it under control, but in the end it controlled him and ruined his life. Homes have been lost in a fleeting moment of weakness. Kingdoms have been bartered for a fleeting moment of pleasure, and an eternal heritage has been squandered for an hour's diversion.

The Bible says, "Be not deceived; God is not mocked: for whatsoever a man soweth, that shall he also reap. For he that soweth to his flesh shall of the flesh reap corruption . . .".

Ref: TITUS 3:3; PROVERBS 14:9; GALATIANS 6:7, 8

Revolution, restlessness and lawlessness often flame so furiously throughout the world that many wonder how we get from week to week without world conflagration. The Scriptures teach that "he who restrains will restrain, until he be taken out of the way." If it were not for the hindering power of the Holy Spirit, we would be engulfed already in the floods of anarchy and corruption. We who trust in Jesus Christ for our salvation do not despair or panic in the face of these threatenings, for we believe that before the final storm breaks the Lord will receive his own unto himself.

Ref: II THESSALONIANS 2:7

TITUS 3:3

For we ourselves also were sometimes foolish, disobedient, deceived, serving divers lusts and pleasures, living in malice and envy, hateful, and hating one another.

PROVERBS 14:9

Fools make a mock at sin: but among the righteous there is favour.

GALATIANS 6:7, 8

Be not deceived; God is not mocked: for whatsoever a man soweth, that shall he also reap.

For he that soweth to his flesh, shall of the flesh reap corruption; but he that soweth to the Spirit, shall of the Spirit reap life everlasting.

II THESSALONIANS 2:7

For the mystery of iniquity doth already work: only he who now letteth, will let, until he be taken out of the way.

Faith is clearly defined in the Bible: "Now faith is the substance of things hoped for, the evidence of things not seen." Faith implies four things: self-renunciation, reliance with utter confidence, obedience and a changed life.

Ref: HEBREWS 11:1

In the book of Acts the Philippian jailer asked the Apostle Paul: "What must I do to be saved?" Paul gave him a straight answer: "Believe on the Lord Jesus Christ, and thou shalt be saved." This is so elementary that millions stumble over it. The one and only choice by which you can be converted is your choice to believe on the Lord Jesus as your own personal Lord and Savior.

You don't have to straighten out your life first. You don't have to make things right at home or in your business first.

Ref: ACTS 16:30, 31

We should shun hell because of God's warnings concerning it. God does not waste time in idle chatter. He makes every word count, and we do well to heed his tender, loving warnings. His Word says, "For if God spared not the angels that sinned, but cast them down to hell, and delivered them into chains of darkness, to be reserved unto judgment, and spared not the old world, but saved Noah the eighth person, a preacher of righteousness, bringing in the flood upon the world of the ungodly . . . The Lord knoweth how . . . to reserve the unjust unto the day of judgment to be punished."

Ref: II PETER 2:4–9

HEBREWS 11:1

Now faith is the substance of things hoped for, the evidence of things not seen.

ACTS 16:30, 31

And brought them out, and said, Sirs, what must I do to be saved;

And they said, Believe on the Lord Jesus Christ, and thou shalt be saved, and thy house.

II PETER 2:4–9

For if God spared not the angels that sinned, but cast them down to hell, and delivered them into chains of darkness, to be reserved unto judgment;

And spared not the old world, but saved Noah, the eighth person, a preacher of righteousness, bringing in the flood upon the world of the ungodly;

And turning the cities of Sodom and Gomorrah into ashes, condemned them with an overthrow, making them an ensample unto those that after should live ungodly;

And delivered just Lot, vexed with the filthy conversation of the wicked;

(For that righteous man dwelling among them, in seeing hearing, vexed his righteous soul from day to day with their unlawful deeds;)

The Lord knoweth how to deliver the godly out of temptations, and to reserve the unjust unto the day of judgment to be punished:

The message of Jesus Christ, our Savior, is the story of the Bible — it is the story of salvation; it is the story of the Gospel; it is the story of life, peace, eternity and heaven. The whole world ought to know the story of the Bible. But if this Gospel is hid today from any American reading these words, it is hidden because you have never opened your Bible; or you have opened it, but with a closed mind.

The Apostle Peter summed it up when he wrote, "The long-suffering of our Lord is salvation; even as our beloved brother Paul also according to the wisdom given unto him has written unto you; as also in all his epistles, speaking in them of these things; in which are some things hard to be understood, which they that are unlearned and unstable wrest, as they do also the other scriptures, unto their own destruction."

Ref: II PETER 3:15, 16

"At the coming of the day of God, the heavens being on fire shall be dissolved, and the elements shall melt with fervent heat. Nevertheless we, according to his promise, look for new heavens and a new earth, wherein dwelleth righteousness. Wherefore, beloved, seeing that ye look for such things, be diligent that ye may be found of him in peace, without spot, and blameless."

There is no time to lose; it is later than you think.

Ref: II PETER 3:11–14

II PETER 3:15, 16

And account that the long-suffering of our Lord is salvation; even as our beloved brother Paul also, according to the wisdom given unto him, hath written unto you;

As also in all his epistles, speaking in them of these things; in which are some things hard to be understood, which they that are unlearned and unstable wrest, as they do also the other scriptures, unto their own destruction.

II PETER 3:11–14

Seeing then that these things shall be dissolved, what manner of persons ought ye to be in all holy conversation and godliness;

Looking for and hasting unto the coming of the day of God, wherein the heavens, being on fire, shall be dissolved, and the elements shall melt with fervent heat?

Nevertheless we, according to his promise, look for new heavens and a new earth, wherein dwelleth righteousness.

Wherefore, beloved, seeing that ye look for such things, be diligent that ye may be found of him in peace, without spot, and blameless.

The Bible teaches, that "the wisdom that is from above is first pure, then peaceable, gentle, and easy to be intreated, full of mercy and good fruits, without partiality, and without hypocrisy."

We are teaching thousands of young people in this country knowledge; but we are not helping them to know how to use that knowledge. In every area of life people are floundering, suffering from neuroses and psychological problems on a scale that we have never known before. Our heads are empty. We have educated people without indicating the source of wisdom, and we have sent them out into the world confused, bewildered and frustrated, without moral moorings.

Ref: JAMES 3:17

Also, Christians suffer in order that God might bring them to repentance. God says, "As many as I love, I rebuke and chasten: be zealous, therefore, and repent." Many Christians make light of sin and have little godly sorrow for sin. God rebukes them in order that they may repent of their sin. If there is sin in your life as a Christian, I urge you to confess it now before the chastening hand of God falls. "If we would judge ourselves, we should not be judged."

Ref: REVELATION 3:19; I CORINTHIANS 11:31

The Apostle Peter, who had suffered intense persecution and hardship in his day, gives us the first answer. He writes: ". . . casting all your care upon Him; for He careth for you." Someone has said that we all carry three loads in life. First, the past, which is full of guilt, unhappy memories, and neglected duties. Second, the present which is filled with the worries and anxieties of everyday life. Third, the future which holds for us fear, terrors, and dreads.

Ref: I PETER 5:7

JAMES 3:17

But the wisdom that is from above is first pure, then peaceable, gentle, and easy to be entreated, full of mercy and good fruits, without partiality, and without hypocrisy.

REVELATION 3:19

As many as I love, I rebuke and chasten: be zealous therefore, and repent.

I CORINTHIANS 11:31

For if we would judge ourselves, we should not be judged.

I PETER 5:7

Casting all your care upon him, for he careth for you.

The subject of the coming again of Christ has never been popular to any but the true believer. We who believe in the return of Christ as taught in the Scriptures should not be surprised that we are unpopular with scoffers. We are warned in the Scriptures that in the last days scoffers will come, saying: "Where is the promise of his coming? for since the fathers fell asleep, all things continue as they were from the beginning of the creation." We must expect to be greeted in many quarters as representatives of an incredible world view. We must expect to be smiled at indulgently by many who consider us interesting cases of arrested development. However, regardless of the opinions of many, there are thousands of us in the world who take our Bibles seriously.

Ref: PETER 3:4

The tongue is to be brought under control. The Bible says, "And the tongue is a fire, a world of iniquity; so is the tongue among our members, that it defileth the whole body, and setteth on fire the course of nature; and it is set on fire of hell."

There are pillows wet by tears, there are hearts needlessly broken, there are noble people hurt and harmed, there are friends separated and lonely, there are chasms opened deep and wide, by cruel tongues—even in the church. We should ask ourselves three questions before we speak: Is it true? Is it kind? Does it glorify Christ? If we did, even speaking would diminish and there would soon be a spiritual awakening that would sweep the church.

Ref: JAMES 3:6

PETER 3:4

And saying, Where is the promise of his coming? for since the fathers fell asleep, all things continue as they were from the beginning of the creation.

JAMES 3:6

And the tongue is a fire, a world of iniquity; so is the tongue among our members, that it defileth the whole body, and setteth on fire the course of nature; and it is set on fire of hell.

Have your time of prayer and your time of Bible reading, and above all discipline your mind. The Bible says much about the mind. "Thou wilt keep him in perfect peace whose mind is stayed on thee." Get your mind in the habit of dwelling on the person of Christ.

Let him take your tongue and nail it to the cross. The Scripture says that we smite with the tongue. "And the tongue is a fire, a world of iniquity: so is the tongue among our members, that it defileth the whole body, and setteth on fire the course of nature; and it is set on fire of hell." Take this little muscle of yours and nail it to the cross.

Ref: JAMES 3:6

Recognize that temptation is a normal experience. The Bible says that temptation has not taken you in any way that is not common to humanity in general. It is a part of our ordinary human experience. Christ, as the only perfect human, was in every respect tempted as we are. Moreover, he felt deeply the spiritual and mental anguish that temptation occasions, for it is written that "he himself hath suffered being tempted."

Ref: HEBREWS 2:18

God chastens Christians not only to bring them to repentance but to train them. The Scripture says, "For whom the Lord loveth he chasteneth, and scourgeth every son whom he receiveth."

I have five children, and many times we have to discipline them for their own good in order to train them.

Ref: HEBREWS 12:6

JAMES 3:6

And the tongue is a fire, a world of iniquity; so is the tongue among our members, that it defileth the whole body and setteth on fire the course of nature; and it is set on fire of hell.

HEBREWS 2:18

For in that he himself hath suffered being tempted, he is able to succour them that are tempted.

HEBREWS 12:6

For whom the Lord loveth he chasteneth, and scourgeth every son whom he receiveth.

The Bible has other fearful descriptions concerning the awful condition in which the soul without Christ will find itself after death. Yet we will prepare for everything except death. We prepare for education; we prepare for business; we prepare for our careers; we prepare for marriage; we prepare for old age; we prepare for everything except the moment we are to die. But the Bible says, "It is appointed unto men once to die."

Ref: HEBREWS 9:27

The Scripture says, "What is your life? It is even a vapor, that appeareth for a little time, and then vanisheth away." Many a person who is cynical and secular has thought deeply about life and eternity. I am convinced that if people gave more thought to death, eternity and judgment, there would be more holy living and a greater consciousness of God.

Ref: JAMES 4:14

HEBREWS 9:27

And as it is appointed unto men once to die, but after this the judgment.

JAMES 4:14

Whereas ye know not what shall be on the morrow. For what is your life? It is even a vapour, that appeareth for a little time, and then vanisheth away.

ABOUT THE AUTHOR

Trudy S. Settel was a Restaurant Columnist for New York's CUE Magazine and also served as a Syndicated Columnist for many years. She has written and edited ten books including *The Light and the Rock, The Book of Ghandi Wisdom, The Faith of JFK* and *Close to Home Auto Tours*.

Ms. Settel was a Vice-President and Editor-in-Chief at Dorison House, a New York Book Publishing Company. Currently, in addition to writing books, she works as a Literary Agent, evaluating and editing manuscripts. She also assists in producing and evaluating lectures on the Golden Age of Radio for Cruise Lines and Libraries throughout the country.